NO LANGUAGE
BUT A CRY

 *NO*

LANGUAGE BUT A CRY

by Richard D'Ambrosio

DOUBLEDAY & COMPANY, INC.
Garden City, New York

Library of Congress Catalog Card Number 75-111154
Copyright © 1970 by Richard D'Ambrosio
All Rights Reserved
Printed in the United States of America

TO
MY MOTHER
AND
FATHER

ACKNOWLEDGMENTS

The author wishes to thank Geoffrey Wagner for a helping hand in the writing of this book, and Estelle Gerard for some diligent typing.

R. D'A.

So runs my dream: but what am I?
An infant crying in the night:
An infant crying for the light:
And with no language but a cry.

Tennyson, *In Memoriam*

PROLOGUE

This is the story of a girl.

Of a baby who was fried alive in a common frying pan at the age of one and a half years, and virtually abandoned as so much human refuse thereafter. Who did not speak for some twelve years of her life.

It is a true story—the names have, of course, been altered—and though unique of its kind, its like happens all too often in our cities. The records of child-caring clinics and institutions can attest to that. I have called the girl Laura.

As I look out of my office now, over stone war memorials shining bladelike in the sun, I realize that Laura's story is so much more. These memorials to the dead remind me that there are no medals to honor those who daily lose the struggle against mental illness and despair, which so afflicted Laura, let alone commemorate the others whose glowing strength of compassion brought her back at last into our world of so-called sanity, and speech. Mental illness fills almost more hospital beds in America than all other known physical and emotional illnesses combined, and child abuse has by now become such a major city problem that mayors assign "task forces" to deal with it.

Laura's task force was a small group of women who refused to accept failure and, in the heart—or cold depths—of the largest metropolitan center the world has ever known, continued to operate on something called faith. Laura was saved by a group of maverick nuns, and so this is their story almost as much as it is hers. More than all that, it is, in embryo, a little history of what it means to be human.

As I write these words the telephone rings. My thoughts are interrupted by the multiple problems of patients, present and absent. A social worker tells me once more about Michael, aged seventeen, depressed, lonely, deprived of family and job, the end of the line . . . Philip, also seventeen, recently committed to a state hospital for the mentally ill after a violent suicide attempt . . . dark-haired Helen, eleven, bright and sensitive but perpetually vomiting, and so unable to attend school.

Each name has a story, just as each face hurrying past into the subway or along the street of a morning carries the stamp of some particular individuality.

So, why Laura? Why was Laura so important to me that I spent years of my life writing up her memory, not to mention guiding her treatment?

Laura meant something for me, and although so many years have passed since first I met her, hunched, scarred, ugly, and afraid, and above all mute, a special feeling still stirs within me whenever I think of her.

In the first place the crossing of our paths was somewhat implausible. At that time I was just beginning to develop a private practice. I was growing confident in my profession, my skills were sharpening, my reputation beginning to develop. It was a time when I was hoping to reap the harvest of long years of study. My available time was limited, precious. Like other analysts, I tended to sense rewards in those most able to profit from the help I could give; the wounds, or traumata, of suffering derived from poverty and social deprivation too often remain an unlikely target for our professional interests.

Laura altered this. It is not for an analyst to analyze himself in public, I imagine, but looking back on the story that follows it is hard for me not to feel there was some strange arrangement of the fates in this meeting. At the time of which I am writing, mental illness for the poor, for those in our urban ghettoes, meant shock therapy, drugs, hospitalization— rather than psychotherapy or psychoanalysis. And perhaps it was the hidden energy of some conflict within me that became the catalyst and driving force converting a perfunctory visit to a gloomy institution into a shattering involvement with the darkest recesses of a child's wounded mind. Of this let the reader be the judge. At some point, at any rate, each of us is brought into some form of stark confrontation with his past, consciously or unconsciously.

Such must remain outside, or on the borders of, Laura's story and that of the nuns. But I might perhaps be permitted to clarify here that these disturbed and helpless children of the very poor, housed in the Institution of which I write, were no strangers to one who had known what it felt like to be poor. For the poor family, money becomes the magic of dreams, and the serpent of nightmares. "If only we had more money . . ." Thus among the poor submission becomes encouraged, since it makes them less disturbing to others, a submission that so easily winds into despair. The meek shall inherit the earth—which turns out to be a surprisingly expensive commodity when you have to buy six feet of it, as you die.

When I first contacted the Institution of this story, I was no longer poor. I was one of the lucky ones, the winners. Those in the Institution were the losers. With the result that the place compelled me from the first with a blind feeling I can really only identify as a sort of loyalty. There but for the grace of God . . .

This is an odd allegiance, yet a man cannot escape from himself and I knew perfectly well that to turn from the confrontation with Laura, and her kin, would have meant for me an abandonment and dereliction of duty. As a child I had frequently felt that the rest of the world had neglected and forgotten the poor. How could I do to others what I felt had been done to me? Every time I rubbed against those infants in the Institution I gulped, and remembered. No money will appease this feeling. One has to face the source of anger, question the sincerity of one's compassion, and take a hard look at whether one can ask more of others than one is willing to give oneself.

To be concrete: there came that moment when I closed Laura's case history, and held it in my hands, and sat and thought. And remembered that there had been a moment in my own youth when a young math teacher, with steel-rimmed spectacles, literally held my own life in his hands in the same way. Because of his decision to get involved in my life, he dramatically helped it forward.

This overworked and underpaid young man had been conducting an after-hours remedial math class when I strolled into his room one Thursday afternoon. And for three months thereafter I sat with him every Tuesday and Thursday at the same time. I was diligent and interested and did everything Mr. Scott told me until there came that day when we walked a corridor together and he inquired about my overall grade in school. An innocuous question but one I preferred to answer only to my parents, accompanied by a bit of rank bravado. It was out of sheer embarrassment that I did not answer Mr. Scott that day, but instead led him a few steps down the hall, clutched his chalk-marked coat, and pointed out the room.

"This is your class?" he asked, adding, in surprise, "You're quite sure?"

I nodded and said nothing. Mr. Scott looked at me in disbelief, then pushed by me and inquired of the teacher standing there.

"Yes," said Miss Stark coldly, "he is one of mine."

It was at our next meeting that Mr. Scott put it to me directly. "Why are you in that class?"

I knew what he meant, and mumbled, "You mean . . . in a class for retarded kids?"

6

"Yes."

It had to come out. I had been placed in the infamous C.R.M.D., an abbreviation for Class for Retarded in Mental Development.

When I first met her, Laura could not even speak.

My own troubles had started, I believe, in third grade when my teacher became exasperated by my failure to learn to read. A very proper Bostonian, she frequently regaled us with stories about plays, operas, and the museums she visited on weekends. She began writing home to my parents, demanding that they help, letters to which the principal in due course added. The trouble was, this meticulous correspondence was rather lost on my parents, who needed a translator since they didn't speak English, were extremely poor, and had seven children to feed and rear. Everyone in the family was working hard, struggling to keep head above water, having mostly been brought to this country from Italy at over the age of thirteen. For a proud family it wasn't easy. We lived in a ghetto that by present-day standards of ghettoes was, well, a ghetto.

So, frozen in my chair, confused, angered yet obedient, I sat in my "retarded" class watching other children throwing themselves on the floor in convulsions instead of pasting cut-outs. I was ostracized, and ridiculed, by both parties—that is to say, the "normal" and the "mentally retarded." Many bloody battles resulted and most days I ran all the way home from school.

How clearly I remember telling my parents about that change in class. How distinctly I recall that helpless acceptance in their faces—were we not poor, and what could the poor do about it?

Mr. Scott promised to try to help. I had no reason to trust him, particularly since he was a teacher, but I liked Mr. Scott. All he said was, "You need help and I want to help you."

For more than six months he gave up hours of his life

7

to tutor me patiently in fourth- and fifth-grade subjects. More than that, he became a friend, someone I could trust. As later I had to try to get Laura to trust me.

One day I was summoned to the principal's office, where Mr. Scott had evidently been striving to convince her of my achievement. As I entered, she was citing the Board of Education bible on rules and regulations. Without warning she placed a reader in my palm and told me to go ahead, read. The words simply stuck in my gullet, until triumphantly she turned to my intercessor and said, "You see, Mr. Scott, you are wasting your time."

All at once that diffident, untidy man with the shiny spectacles shuffled close to me and begged me to read what I saw. Suddenly I began; the words flowed easily. Later, when he started to question me on the subjects I had studied, my thoughts were clear, my responses correct.

So I was taken out of C.R.M.D. and placed in fifth grade "on trial." The next step was that I got the highest mark in the school in the city-wide arithmetic test. I repeated the achievement in eighth grade, much to the amazement of the principal. Mr. Scott began to tutor me, still gratuitously, in algebra, after which I asked permission to take the entrance examination for the three special high schools of science in the city, a step that Mr. Scott warned me, rightly as it turned out, would infuriate the principal. For her I was still "mentally retarded." Eventually, after due drama, I was allowed to be one of three from the school who took the exam. Two passed. I was one of them.

Many years later, when I progressed successfully through my doctoral studies, Mr. Scott faded from my life. What he is doing now I do not know, but wherever he may be I raise my hat to him. He gave me a helping hand out of despair. Perhaps, if he had not extended that chalk-dusty palm to me in those days, I should have been condemned forever as a young defective, on the simple basis of language handicap.

The major difference, obviously enough, between my life

and Laura's was that I had escaped and she was still trapped. I was a winner and she a loser. True, there were not the same basic problems, but I am here trying to assess that surge of anger and desire which forced me to give battle, almost against my reason, on behalf of an unknown mute girl, and fight the common enemy of prejudice and ignorance in that power structure known as society, where the poor never forget that they are poor, and are often thought of as "defective."

At first my commitment seemed small and with a definite end in sight. I would indeed have achieved my goal if I had given my professional attention to one or more of the disturbed children in the Institution who were hungry for affection and in need of someone with whom to talk. My feelings rose as I began to see the possibility that in a year at most I would have carried out my personal mission and pledge, and could resume with full energy my own ambition. Instead I stayed ten years. The fates had their own plans, their own drama to unfold, and so it was that a mute child called Laura, whose lips seemed forever locked in silence, made a mockery of everything I knew as an analyst and challenged all I was as a person.

Laura's story starts truly in the emergency ward of a crowded city hospital one cold October evening when the siren of a police ambulance cut through snarled traffic and a cop with bulging eyes and drooping lower lip helped carry his stretcher onto the wheeled roller where lay a very small bundle of humanity.

"Seffen seffen seffen, in Emergency," a woman's voice was saying, as the roller was wheeled to the operating room. "Seffen seffen sef-fen . . . in Emergency."

Fifty percent of the barely year-old body was covered with second-degree burns. All the way to Emergency the cop had had the smell of charred flesh in his nostrils and frankly he wondered if he'd ever get it out again. He was trying not to see those lips blown tight, bloated like some . . . some golden raisin.

All this I pieced together, in bits and fragments, as I reconstructed Laura's life later. The question at that moment was, would she make it? I talked to the girl clerk who had been the one checking records in her small windowed office in the hospital that night. As they gave Laura plasma, the cop had chatted with the clerk as he filled out his forms. It was not the first time he had done so. Accustomed as the clerk was even then to a litany of nightly human misery, she had looked up sharply when the cop told her that the infant had been cooked alive—"placed in a large frying pan by her parents and fried alive on an open flame."

Later the clerk accompanied the policeman back to his ambulance. The cop had paused, panting, by a water fountain stuck with gum and flowing in old spittle. He told her that the child's parents lived in a railroad flat over a bakery. That the neighbors continually complained about the kid screaming. "She cries too much" was the father's explanation for his action. A drinker, as is often true in these cases, and one who went in for killing cats. He had been reported for pouring gasoline on one, and setting it alight.

The girl had asked the child's name. Laura. As they talked, another stretcher was already being wheeled up the incline, carrying a tall, light-skinned Negro on his back in a soiled raincoat, his chest heaving.

"I got to go call my wife," the cop had said, digging into a pocket for a dime.

Inside the hospital, a girl child named Laura, with an unbelievably burned and welted body, fought for life.

Part One

LANGUAGE

1

If for Laura her story began in ghastly and inchoate drama, for me it started innocently enough aboard an Eastern Airlines flight on which I was returning from a Thanksgiving convention in Chicago.

I had given a talk on mental health and on the plane flight back found myself seated next to the attractive young lady who had acted as chairman of my special seminar.

Dorothy had crossed my path in graduate school once or twice, but I could not say I knew her well. However, as we chatted, relaxing after the professional tensions abounding at such meetings, I found we had a lot in common. She had grown up in an area of the city I knew well and was now, it seemed, a social worker.

"Where?" I asked incuriously.

"A couple of institutions," she explained. She glanced at me tentatively. "One of them's for girls."

"Oh."

"Actually, I don't really work in them. I'm connected with their main office. I do the paper work, budgets, hiring staff, so on."

"Sounds like interesting work," I commented without much enthusiasm.

Frankly the very word "institution" repelled me.

I had gone into psychoanalysis in a desire to understand the workings of the human mind, to get closer to the feelings and relationships that exist between individuals. I had already begun to build up a small but promising practice, was intensely interested in my "analysands" and was learning from them as I hoped they were from me. The idea of an institution seemed cold, detached, the antithesis of that close communication between individuals I was interested in.

"There are about a hundred and fifty girls there," Dorothy explained to me, as we sipped our coffee together, "almost all from broken homes, and of all ages up to eighteen."

I hummed politely. City agencies did not generally provide care for girls over eighteen. And the story was familiar: alcoholic parents, abandoned children, disrupted marriages, the mentally and physically sick. When the FASTEN YOUR SEAT BELT signs flashed on somewhere over New York, I was surprised to find Dorothy looking at me with a quizzical smile and saying, "It's a promise, then?"

"What is?"

"You will come?"

Evidently I had made one of those half-conscious agreements during our small talk. The girl was thoroughly determined to take me out to see one of her institutions, that for girls, and by the time we touched down I had—rather grouchily, I confess—settled on a date.

It was a bitterly cold December day when Dorothy picked me up in her battered Chevvy and drove me over the bridge out of Manhattan. Snow slipped at us in flurries, the river was a surly gray.

As we drove, my mood did not improve. Dorothy was making for a particularly depressing neighborhood, one of tenements and projects where only a fleeting face was seen at a window. This dismal sprawl of the city filled me with gloom—old people shuffling past subway gratings, dime stores with broken panes, rundown cafeterias and automats, occasionally tiny railed parks where, I imagined, expressionless figures would sit all summer, moving their hands and spitting. While she drove, she talked.

"I work at the Institutional Field Office," she said, adding a little timidly, "These two places are both under Catholic sponsorship."

"Not controlled by the city?" I asked.

"The Department of Welfare does contribute some money, but it's the local Catholic Charities that are almost entirely responsible, for the children's food, shelter, clothing. The nuns act as 'group mothers,' sort of substitute mothers. They try hard but there are so many children for them to take care of."

"Any intensive psychological help available?"

The sky seemed blocked by stone. These dilapidated buildings, and rusting fire escapes, and blind windows, and the strayed garbage pails on vacant lots, were already getting under my skin. I began to know why I had avoided coming into these neighborhoods. There is something infinitely life-destroying about the end of the American city, when it peters out into these drab shopfronts and forgotten counters.

"No. There's only us social workers in that line," my companion told me. "But here we are." She braked to park. Almost offhandedly she added, "And there's the Institution."

The snow was falling in thick wet flakes, making the street we'd pulled up in look somehow dark and shadowy. Dorothy switched off the ignition. Across from us I could discern a massive gathering of stone, a sort of colorless accumulation of mortar, stretching for an entire block. It was a block. My first thought was that it was a prison, a kind of junior Bastille, ugly and uninviting.

This soulless barrack—brick upon brick of it—seemed to drain all vitality out of me as I crossed the street after my friend. Quickening my steps through the snow, I saw suddenly that the huge mass was further protected by rows of barbed wire along the outer walls, to which had been cemented what appeared to be bits of broken glass and old, sharply spiked gaffs.

The stone stairs we mounted in front of these sullen walls

seemed endless. I tugged an iron bell pull with all my strength and a nineteenth-century knell seemed to shiver through my marrow. After what seemed an eternity the great door swung wide and a smiling, almost laughing, nun invited us to enter.

As I did so, stamping the snow off my rubbers in the hallway, I remembered how we had kidded at exams at college—"Abandon hope, all ye who enter here." Dorothy and I followed the black-robed nun down a lengthy corridor, in which the sound of singing voices could be faintly heard. On either side I noticed freshly painted rooms and gay decorations. Intermittently we could hear children talking with animation and giggling. On the walls were bulletin boards, one of which described the activities scheduled for the girls that week. In a niche at the end of the corridor stood a huge statue of a saint with outstretched arms.

The nun was leading us, I understood, to the superintendent's office. Watching her white collar, and the black robes that wobbled wildly from side to side as she walked, I whispered to Dorothy, "Just like a penguin." She smiled and motioned for me to behave myself.

Then a group of tiny children charged out of a room, struggling with each other and laughing. Two of them kept pace with us, clinging to my arm, and reaching up for me to touch, until the penguin smilingly reproved them and told them to go back. I was aware of a faint white smell, but couldn't for the life of me identify it.

In her dignified, paneled office the superintendent rose to greet us. She was a tall, square-shouldered woman, by no means old and by no means plain, despite her lack of all makeup. She chatted with Dorothy a while, mostly about local problems, then turned to me. "I am so glad you came. So many disturbed children here need intensive help beyond what we and the social workers can give them. But come, let me show you around."

We began to tour the Institution.

The children from two to five lived in the basement. In each dormitory were ten to twelve youngsters, all neatly dressed, with tidy braids tied in pretty ribbons.

All along these dormitories the children ran up to me in happy spontaneity, grabbing, holding and pulling, asking to be lifted or touched, asking to be held, crying out. The penguin nun shushed them in vain, whispering on the side that the littlest children needed so much attention.

It was as we walked through the nursery that the odor I had noticed became definable. It was milk, a symbolic reminder that here were those who lived without their mothers —or fathers or families, for that matter—outcasts of society. Years ago, I was told, the Institution had been an orphanage.

From this floor we took the elevator to the second. As the doors clashed wide we were greeted with a babel of singing and laughing, groups of children being busy making paperchains, decorations, and the like. Their irrepressible liveliness was underlined, sadly enough, as we passed on into the infirmary, where a ten-year-old child with large eyes and thin bones lay in bed.

"She's waiting for a doctor to find time to come," Dorothy told me, while the two robed figures tried to cheer the youngster. "I'm afraid Clare's temperature's still quite high."

The girl's great eyes hung on mine. I suppose it was because she had never seen me before that she stared with such painful concentration. I searched for something comforting to say, something to make her happier and myself less . . . responsible.

"You'll be better soon, Clare."

I hated the words the moment they left my lips. The meaningless cliché did not stop the fixity of her stare any more than, in reality, I had expected it to. I patted Clare's feet. They looked oddly large, under the blanket.

Her eyes followed mine with an adult intelligence. Those eyes knew, better than I could, all about loneliness.

And indeed, as if reading my thoughts, Dorothy said, "We've tried and tried, but we haven't been able to find Clare's family."

I commented briefly to the nun, walking with us in the corridor now, that children like Clare must at times find life a hard burden, must even wonder if the struggle was really worth the effort.

"That's just it, Doctor." She nodded at once, and explained that, like most of the children in the Institution, Clare was especially vulnerable when ill for that very reason: because their will to live is diminished by their intense loneliness, and even despair, at the lack of family love in such moments.

We were now walking into the dormitories where as many as twenty-five girls lived together. Each had a bed, a large closet, and the rooms were all decorated with attractive curtains and bedspreads. Without exception there was a stuffed animal or doll on every bed.

I was told that the girls in these dormitories ranged in age from five through twelve or so; they cared for their own beds, had their own dining room, washed their dishes, and every now and then—at their own request—vied with each other to do some mouth-watering cooking in the huge communal kitchen.

Each division was headed by a nun, with a number of lay assistants who helped care for the girls. As we returned to the elevator the superintendent mentioned that the third floor was divided into apartments for the adolescent girls, who were at present out, attending high school in the community. We had reached the main floor again.

"We should like to thank you for coming, Doctor," said the superintendent finally. Her pale eyes studied me closely.

"Yes, thank you, Doctor," said the nun who throughout our tour had shown considerable deference to her superior.

"We don't suffer from an excess of attention from the outside world," the superintendent said in the same level tone.

Perhaps she was watching to see how I would take the comment. Was it one made to all of us who lived on the outside and pretended that institutions were always someone else's concern? A saying came to my mind: "It is easier to love humanity as a whole than to love one's neighbor." Was she pointing a finger at me, or was I accusing myself of indifference to this "other" side of humanity? Yet, I didn't feel indifferent. There was something in the faces of the children, in the sight of their exposed knees, in Clare's large eyes that tugged deeply at my emotions. But she must have been used enough to the attitude, for there was a certain cynicism in her tone. As I thought about the overwhelming forces these nuns were fighting, I began for the first time to understand their courage.

"About what portion, Sister, are emotionally disturbed?" I asked.

"At least a third," the superintendent answered. "Perhaps half."

They were all three watching me. I realized that.

Suddenly there was a flow of children from somewhere, nowhere, pelting down the passage, laughing and calling after each other, and for a second—before the nun in charge had caught up with them—threatening to engulf us in wind-milling arms and flying braids.

One dark girl with silky hair got left behind, and remained clinging to my arm, smiling up at me with that shy but wistfully knowledgeable look some children have.

The superintendent chose this moment to ask, "And do you think you'd be visiting us again perhaps, Doctor?"

"At the moment it doesn't look as if I'm going to be allowed to get away, does it?" I looked down at the tot, who, with a pat, was sent on her way by the nun.

"Whenever you'd like to. You have only to let Dorothy know."

The tall woman smiled again, gave me that karate handshake of hers, and murmured, "God bless you." She turned and left us.

A minute later I was walking down the cold wet steps with my friend. The great door of the Institution closed firmly behind us. The snow had risen to a storm, which struck us with full force as we stood there a moment, collecting ourselves to cross the street.

Whipped with white, the street was wider than I'd remembered, needlessly large. Or so it seemed to me, as I struggled to get across it, back to the car. A bus groaned by, splashing my ankles. But as I moved effortfully through these whorls and gusts I felt only fingers tugging, hands clasping. And I smelled milk.

As I got in the old jalopy and Dorothy started its reluctant engine, I hoped she wasn't going to talk about foster homes and . . . institutions. She must have sensed my mood, for she said nothing. And I said nothing, either, my mind full in the snowy sky of a child's big eyes, and thin bones under the blankets.

"Each one of them—" I started once, then broke off.

At that point I wasn't sure of myself. I was tired and eager to get home. But throughout the trip my thoughts kept returning to the children, and the nuns. The whole thing was silly, I thought; what could a single person do? I had to consider my career and the little enough time I had to devote to my own patients. Maybe I would send the nuns a check, some donation for the children. It would make me feel better.

Around us the traffic began to jam, and hoot. As it hived for the entry to the bridge the city's lights could be seen like so many promises, strings of lanterns magical in the sky, like those decorations . . . then Dorothy was saying, "Do you think you'll come back? I mean . . ." She went on, "I don't have to tell you how much . . ."

"Is there any remuneration involved?"

"Little." She added, "The nuns, of course, work for nothing."

"All right," I returned, gruffly enough, "make it the same time next week, and you don't have to pick me up. I'll find my way alone."

Language

The woman beside me said nothing. She looked ahead, through the strings of steel we were now entering; but when we'd crossed the bridge her chin came up a little. "I'll have the case histories ready for you to read."

As I look back these many years later I can now understand the conflicting feelings passing through my mind as I questioned the wisdom of involving myself with the helpless fragments of humanity thrown together in this Institution. I sometimes think that, faced with the confrontation at that moment, perhaps I was too much of a coward to refuse.

2

A week later I was sitting in a bare office put at my disposal in the Institution and reading its case histories. Curiosity about the lives of the children kept me from wondering why I had ever consented to come.

By nature a psychoanalyst's job brings him into contact with a great deal of unhappiness and mental distortion. But as I stared at each new record before me and tried to puzzle through the lines of data presented, I realize it is rarely in a single lifetime that one comes across such a sheer accumulation of human misery as this.

It was a litany of damaged dreams and lives betrayed. The facts were there, but not the feelings. When dealing with a child, the full impact of life can never be recorded, however accurate the facts. I wondered, for instance, how Nancy had felt when her mother became critically ill and she was placed in a strange, unknown environment. What it must have been like for Susan, exposed week after week, month after month, to a father in an alcoholic rage, lying in bed, fists clenched, dreading his return. Or Anne, striving to make some vague sense out of a mother's hallucinatory or frankly delusional remarks.

Silence surrounded me as I read, broken only by an unusually insistent horn from some double-parked deliverer in the street outside or the subdued, hushed rushing of nuns passing down the passage. Reading on, I found the cases to assume an almost nightmare regularity, or sameness. There was a voice from my past, a colleague with a Park Avenue practice whom I'd overheard saying to a social worker, "Why waste your time on those neglected kids? Middle-class children can profit from psychotherapy, sure, but those deprived cases . . ."

Then one sheet refused to be turned. It was the hospital record of a girl who had been horribly burned, actually cooked in a frying pan. I read on. The girl's charred, almost lifeless body, its arms limply dangling, had been carried into emergency by a policeman. Plasma had been administered at once. Somehow, despite the fact that more than half her body had been severely burned and scarred, she had hung on to life. Swathed in bandages from head to toes she had remained on the hospital's critical list for weeks. The case history continued with an itemization of treatments.

Other records told me that for the first year and a half of her so-called life this infant had been regularly beaten, drubbed, bruised, and mauled by a pair of mentally ill and alcoholic parents.

Whenever a neighbor had chanced on the child she had been found to be a mass of welts from the beatings she'd received. Finally, on the evening in question, one neighbor more compassionate than most had been unable to stand the anguished cries and had called the police. They had had to break in, and there they had found the child being held in a frying pan by her parents, who were calmly cooking her alive. Furthermore, the records before me indicated that this was but half of the problem. Burns can be healed, eventually. Damage to the personality is much harder to cure.

For this creature had had almost every card in the deck stacked against her since her birth some two hours after her inebriated mother had entered the emergency room of another city hospital. Scattered as were the reports, I soon came to realize that it would be easier to describe what was *not* wrong with her.

She had a severe curvature of the spine, her eyes were crossed, and she suffered from—among other things—pronounced varicose veins of the legs. At the age of five she had been diagnosed as suffering from schizophrenia, perhaps the severest form of mental illness, and accordingly referred to a state hospital for the mentally ill.

My hands were stiff as I laid down the pages of cold print and tried to light a cigarette. The lines of a poem I had been given to learn years ago in high school blazed into sudden memory:

> And how am I to face the odds
> Of man's bedevilment and God's?
> I, a stranger and afraid
> In a world I never made.

It was by far the worst case before me. The girl was now aged twelve. She was totally without speech. Her name was Laura.

At this point it may well be asked what happens to a piece of human flotsam when it gets washed up in our cities? Sadly, it is a question all too often presented. The layman has no conception of the extent of suffering behind the walls of our hospitals and, yes, our institutions. Laura was, then, a case in point. A physical anomaly. A social outcast. Human refuse, if you will.

At the time when Laura was initially being cared for in the hospital, her parents were examined in the psychiatric ward. Both were found to have pushed well beyond alcoholism into mental illness, and were recommended to be institutionalized in a state hospital for the mentally ill. Both people of quick, even savage, temper and violence, they resented this institutionalization with intense hostility. From what I could learn it would not be long before they wanted out.

This left little Laura, meanwhile, without any family, since an investigation could turn up only an aunt, the mother's sister, who soon moved and left no forwarding address. Lying on her hospital cot, Laura was classified as a neglected child, a dependent on the care of the city. These technical labels disguised more than they revealed about the nature of her plight.

Once she was physically healed—or should I say repaired as far as possible?—the hospital had been anxious to refer her to a foster home. Yet Laura was scarcely dischargeable, even if—as was most unlikely—a home could have been found for such an unattractive child, such a potential burden. All the hospital (and, later, the children's shelter) reports identified her as lethargic to the point of stupor, unresponsive to any human interest. She ate poorly, seemed thoroughly apathetic, and the nursery staff reported that she was drawn neither to play objects nor her fellow infants, sitting for hours on end on the floor in a trancelike state. The jargon did not deceive me. "She seems to be maturing late in large muscle control" might euphemize the fact that she scarcely moved at all. Worst of all, at five Laura could not speak a word.

Normally, of course, it could be expected that, even given her experiences, the child would have made some moves toward communicating her needs, and certainly by language, by the age of three and a half. This did not happen with Laura. She sat locked in silence. Psychological examination found lack of development, apathy, and an IQ of fifty. She was classified as functioning at the level of a mental defective, some of the doctors believing her lack of response and adaptation to be the direct result of mental deficiency, and others taking the view that there was here an emotional failure to come to any terms with the world, in short—schizophrenia.

So Laura was finally recommended for referral to a state hospital for the mentally ill. If this had taken place, I am confident I should not now be writing these words. The human derelict would have continued such. But at this moment, and for the first time, fate took another tack. No state hospital reached had room in their children's division to accept Laura. This statistic is telling enough tragedy in itself. She was in a limbo of sorts, semantically inexistent.

In desperation, social workers searched through the community and by chance found what I have called the Institution.

As I read, I became curious about the nature of this place and turned to a document concerning it that had been put at my disposal in the office. I learned that it was originally an orphan asylum, a charitable home that took care of abandoned and destitute girls. Through individual contributions the local Catholic Charities provided food, shelter, clothing, and other necessities for the children. As Dorothy had mentioned, the Department of Welfare of the City of New York also contributed significantly.

Interestingly enough, the nuns who worked in the Institution formed a kind of third party in this arrangement, for they belonged neither to the city nor the local Catholic Charities. They were first and foremost members of an order dedicated to child care.

Missionaries of a sort, they were governed by a mother general in Rome, under whose command they were allotted to a position most likely to fulfill the promise of their order. Hence, these nuns were merely on loan, as it were, to the local Catholic Charity; only the order itself received a token payment for their services.

For these, as Dorothy had rightly explained to me, the nuns themselves received nothing. Sworn to chastity, obedience, and poverty, they began their day at 5 A.M. and finished it, if they were lucky, at midnight. Seven days a week.

Whatever the nuns needed, and couldn't make for themselves, from carfare to a new pair of shoes, they were required to kneel before the mother superior and beg for. Should they receive a gift of money, it was turned over to the mother superior at once. Any money the order received for the nuns' services was used to start schools or provide medical supplies for the needy in other parts of the country.

I learned, too, that the type of girl coming into the Institution had changed over the years. There were few orphans now. Instead, most of the children were from broken homes, offspring of the alcoholic, incompetent, mentally or physically sick. The majority of them were, as the superintendent had suggested to me, emotionally disturbed, socially maladjusted, and educationally handicapped. The kids were of all kinds and colors, black, white, yellow. There were Puerto Rican girls as well as Japanese, Chinese, Negro. There were those who had been rescued from Protestant and Jewish, as well as Catholic, homes. If they needed shelter, and help, the nuns took them in.

The reports on Laura were all the same. During her seven years in the Institution she had remained mute, friendless, unresponsive to her peers, untouched by the sympathetic attention of the nuns. In her early period there she had had daily to be fed, washed, clothed. The nuns had had to do everything for her. The girl would sit by herself for hours on end, it seemed, occasionally dangling some toy or doll, but for the most part all too obviously living in a world of her own. Despite all the programs and activities devised for her, her existence had remained almost purely biological.

As I read their records, I was struck by the compassion the nuns had quite gratuitously shown for this . . . human vegetable. Behind their clumsy prose was the hope that one day Laura would be like other children (surely there was hope?) and notes close on despair, too, at lack of any response from her. Above all, I began to sense the group spirit of the place, for it was clear that, though there had been no change in Laura's external behavior, no one wanted to send her away to what so often becomes a kind of living death.

According to the reports, Laura's parents had been admitted, separately, on three different occasions to mental hospitals,

27

both diagnosed as schizophrenic, paranoid types, still potentially dangerous to others. So Laura lived here, perhaps within calling distance of where I was comfortably seated, attending school in the Institution, alone and silent in the back of the room, staring out the window or with her myopic-eyed, squinting face resting on her arms. The teachers of these institutional classes found Laura completely uninvolved in classroom work. They really didn't understand what was wrong with her except that she was shy, withdrawn, and, of course, uncommunicative.

I put the record of this human accident to one side. The sound of childish voices piping something in unison came to me vaguely from somewhere, but I could not identify what it was. I was thinking, assessing. Instead of love, in relation to adults, Laura had known terror; instead of that comfort which comes from being wanted, only deprivation. I was convinced she had suffered a profound shock of a kind that would throw any individual in similar circumstances into the protective world of fantasy. Laura did not want to be hurt again. She wanted to survive. The pages lay there like an accusation.

Standing up, I assembled all the material I had been given by Dorothy. Although I was cold, I realized I was perspiring. I picked up my raincoat and my hat and I looked around the office. Such misery, violence, degradation, sheer atrocity on the part of a mother and father against their infant daughter —was there anything that could be done for her?

From the window I could see a snow-bound street, with slowly churning traffic, and irrelevantly I wondered if I'd beat the rush hour back. Spindly television antennas were planted on rooftops black as slate in the half light. A seamy movie house was visible, its neon garishly discrepant. A brightly lit bus plowed along, on its side a big ad: STRIKE IT RICH . . . WIN THOUSANDS IN OUR NEW . . .

I walked out and closed the door behind me and went down the long corridors to the superintendent's office. She saw me outside and at once beckoned me in. For a second we stood looking at each other, uncertainly.

"Thank you for visiting us, Doctor." Her tongue darted quickly over her lightly downed upper lip. "Did you come across anything that interested you?"

I answered, "I'd like to work with one of your girls."

The pale, big-boned face flushed. Yes, I caught something at that moment that I don't believe I saw again—the superintendent blushed like a schoolgirl. Despite her attempt to disguise the fact, I realized how grateful she was, while I was already wondering about the wisdom of my decision. For a second, remembering her devastating grip, I was afraid the good woman was going to shake my hand again. I took an instinctive pace back. Her face had set into its habitual severity.

"That is, Sister, if I may."

"If you may?" she said wonderingly. "You realize, we can do little to—"

"Of course," I said, almost snappishly.

"Then which," she asked, her clear eyes roving slowly around the paneled room, "just which of our girls did you think, Doctor, you might . . . ?"

I looked long and steadily into those eyes. What I said was, "Laura."

3

Behind me the mammoth gray of the Institution was being lightly downed in snow as I walked to my car. I was looking forward to getting home. I felt I had got myself into enough difficulty for one day.

But I did not drive home.

The high lampposts of the area, like so many dumb giraffes, flickered overhead as I sat behind the wheel and thought. I crossed the river and found myself heading uptown.

Soon I was in an area of vacant lots, doors patched with board, paint-chipped storefronts, and crumbling buildings. I parked between Juanita's Dime Store and something that called itself Luz, Justicia y Verdad, Inc., and which seemed to be selling packages of Fast-Luck Incense. As I wrestled with a meter plugged out of all hope of operation, a woman in a bright-hued coat was calling to her son, *"Dame la mano,* Junior." Perhaps it was only in America, with its rapidity of construction and destruction, that you could turn Park Avenue into a Puerto Rican plaza within a couple of years.

I had to walk east three blocks. Countless phone numbers seemed to have been scrawled on the door of Brazilian Enterprises, whatever that was. Trabajo De Colision (We Do Repairs), no doubt a popular service. Would Laura have made it as one of the "Shangri-La Debs," who announced their next freak-out in the window of El Candy Store? The district might have changed, but the pink stone build-

ing criss-crossed by fire escapes was well kept. There was
the pastry shop I had read about. For this is where it had
happened.

Snow coated the streets thinly, like the confectioners' sugar
on those Italian cakes, cookies, and pastries of my own youth.
Across the street from what had once been Laura's only home
I stood and looked. From somewhere was coming the smell
of freshly baked bread, reminding me of the sense of warmth
you get when you give a child a hug, and which vividly
returned me to my own childhood.

In my boyhood the *cannolo* was by far the most popular
pastry in the *pasticcerìa*, a pie crust fried into a crisp tube—
it was usually shaped around short strips of broom handles
and lowered into boiling oil. After this it was stuffed with a
heavy cream flavored with chocolate and citron. Eating these
after Sunday pasta was, and is, an established ritual among
Italian immigrants and I was on my second *cannolo* before
Jack Di Salvio, the baker, began to open up. He was a short
burly figure whose waistline seemed to make it imperative
for him to hoist up his pants every two or three seconds.
The police blotter for that fatal day in Laura's life had
mentioned the Murtaghs, the Jacowskis, Florence Bernstein
and the Kellys, and a baker, Jack Di Salvio.

The man lived directly over the store with his wife, Anna,
and their six children. As proprietor of the bakery, and landlord of the building, his was just about the richest family in
the block. Why, his wife owned a genuine mink coat. Being
able to speak a southern Italian dialect, I progressed famously
with Jack Di Salvio and could see from the start that the
pink stone building was a source of real pride to him, with
its little fluted arches over each window—"Look just like eye-
brows, is what my daughter Gina always says." And he gave
an expressive heave at his recalcitrant pants.

Originally, it seemed, the place had had twelve dingy apartments, four to each floor above the store. Now he and Anna
and the kids were living like royalty on the second, rail-

roaded. The Kellys and the Murtaghs divided the third between them—"And y'know it, Doc, they scarcely ever fight."

It was almost eleven years ago by now since that big Martin
Meyer and his wife had come into this pastry shop and talked
him into letting them have the left rooms rear, fourth floor,
on the fruit-store side. Seemed like a nice guy. And he himself had wanted to make something on the space. So the couple
and their new baby had moved right in. Not much to move
with them, either. And almost at once Mrs. Bernstein, opposite, had begun to complain about the baby screaming.

"Those were terrible people, the Meyers, they were sick
people . . . like I say, they were strange. . . . I can't tell you
what a terrible thing went on in my house. . . ." With another prodigious hitch at his pants he turned to an incoming
customer. When he rejoined me a moment later he was shaking his curly, gray-haired head. "That poor child."

He didn't want to tell me, but I had to hear. And the lines
I had been reading all afternoon came bitterly to life, as
Jack Di Salvio talked on and on.

I began to see it all. First, the Di Salvio family, particularly
brown-braided Gina, the tomboy, and her kid brother, Mark,
always reading *Captain Marvel*, and having great difficulty
understanding something called "Extreem Unction." The baby
wailing loudly, the cry cutting through the house like a knife,
as the scuffling, laughing Di Salvio children tried to learn
their catechism. Baby Laura, whose cry seemed at times to
slice the very sky, until Gina, or Mark, or Salvatore begged
their mother to get it to quiet.

Then there was Peg Murtagh, in her horticultural hats.
Given, it seemed, to a congenial drop, or nip, with her friend
Marie Kelly of a midmorning. They had tried to help. Peg
Murtagh had declared herself "nervous for that baby" to her
landlord. She had seen the infant's bruises, heard her squalling
when her father had stumbled up the stairs, home after an
all-night drinking bout. And worse. Jack Di Salvio ruffled his
gray-haired crop. Much worse—"The man used to say she

32

cried too much." Oh, there had been complaints enough. But what could he do? He couldn't interfere.

So the lament of the infant's agony had gone on, and on, the cries growing into a crescent scream, or dying to a whine. "That shitbrat" had been the favorite epithet of the man with the bewildered eyes and great gnarled hands who was her father. And then, and then . . .

According to Di Salvio, it had been Mrs. Bernstein who had first given the alarm. A lonely widow, who had lost a daughter to polio some twenty years before, and whose grave she tended in Queens each Sunday, Mrs. Bernstein used to sit at her window in the evening and watch the gap between the weather-stained tenements grow ruddy, as the sun vanished out of sight, out of her reach, somewhere beyond the Jersey shore. The evening hour, before night's long journey, when the crying got the worst.

That night the baby's cry changed completely. Or so it had seemed to Mrs. Bernstein, hauled to her feet by the frantic animality of the sound scalding through the air about her. Something inside, so she had told Di Salvio later, had told her that this uninterrupted scream had gone beyond all urgency, had turned into a matter of life and death. So she had flung up the sash of her window and yelled for the police.

Jack Di Salvio heard her. Who couldn't? "This sixty-year-old woman hanging out the window up there, yelling her lungs out into the street. My family come spilling into the store. Me, I get the cop. He was right across there, Doc, in the Civic Club opposite . . ."

By the time the cop, with bulging eyes and drooping lower lip, and the Di Salvios and the Kellys and Murtaghs, had reached the fourth floor, Laura Meyer was mercifully silent. The cop rapped on the door with his billy and Florence Bernstein, it seemed, had said stiffly in the silence, "They are killing a baby inside."

In a single thudding rush the cop beat in the door. It was

Gina Di Salvio who was right behind him and who, when they reached the kitchen, gave the first scream. In the hot and smoky frying pan, black and red and pasty white, lay a baby girl, her lips pursed tight like a golden raisin.

4

The week passed curiously slowly. After my talk with Jack Di Salvio my mind was full of Laura. Between patients I would find myself thinking about her, and her parents. In the back of a taxicab, at the wheel of my car, in some crowded subway, or a telephone booth, her name would come to me.

I began to speculate. I wondered if I would ever be able to put the puzzle together. Could she speak, or was she forever emotionally blocked from talking? I really didn't know but I began making notes, based on three fairly clear aspects of her case.

First, she was the child of parents whose alcoholism, excesses, and general failure to adapt to life had deprived them of any capacity to love an infant. Laura had been denied the most elementary forms of care essential to the newborn.

Second, at a time when she was barely beginning to differentiate herself from her environment, she was brutally abused and deprived. She had never known a mother's warmth, the feeling of being wanted, the sense of being safe. For her the world she had been born into was hostile and threatening.

Third, at a critical state in her psychological development, she had been hospitalized. This may have freed her from physical torture but, if anything, it had tended to intensify her isolation and abandonment. To be separated from parents at this age is at best a traumatic experience and Laura had been given an additional shock, in her chaotic little career.

The limited staff of a city hospital could never provide the emotional climate she so badly needed at this moment. Her only refuge was to cut herself off completely from the external world around her—what we sometimes call the extensional world—and immure herself within her own fantasies. The schizophrenic individual has great difficulty in distinguishing between the figurative and the factual.

Everything I had read about her added to this impression. A child wants to survive. To do so it must grow increasingly acquainted with reality, and more perceptive of the differences between itself and the world at large. Language is a prime means of organizing our universe sensibly, and a child names things out of love.

But Laura had known no love. Only anxiety, fear of punishment. Rather than having been lured to make contact with the world by love, she had been repulsed from it by hate. "*She cries too much.*" The comment began to echo through my dreams. I began to realize—as I rushed to and fro through the city on my work—that it would be best if I discarded Laura's chronological age from my mind entirely, and thought first and foremost of her psychological age. In this sense, she was an infant. She had scarcely begun to live. Only in this way could I begin to understand her.

Whether something from that strange, sealed group of sisters had rubbed off on me, I don't know. I do know that I became increasingly determined to help Laura.

I said nothing to my secretary, a woman who by now knows my moods intimately. In plain language it wouldn't make sense. Here I was getting involved in the treatment of a deformed, mute girl, diagnosed as schizophrenic *in addition to* being possibly mentally defective, while I should have been spending time developing my own practice.

I was hurrying northward in a howling antique of the IRT when I realized that Laura's fears were clearly stated in the proverb: The burnt child dreads the fire. In Laura's case it had a symbolic as well as a literal meaning; one of her most desperate fears noted at the Institution, a terror amounting to phobia, was that of fire.

Buying my paper at the corner newsstand that freezing morning I was due to go out there again, I said to Abe, the vendor, "How're you doing?"

"Oh, keeping alive, Doc, I guess," he answered in a friendly tone. I wonder if he saw the look his unthinking reply made me give him.

The sky was cold but clear, and since I wanted to do some more thinking I chose to go in a cab. I was finally on my way to see Laura, with nothing more than a few hunches and a lot of unanswered questions. Some cheerful music was playing from the car radio and, as I paid the driver, an announcer cut in with the reminder, "Only eight more shopping days to . . ."

Again I noticed the obliterating bleakness of the neighborhood, but I could feel myself growing self-protectively accustomed to it. The same resonant bell clanged out—as if through the pages of some Gothic novel—and the same nun greeted me inside, leading me off at once in a direction new to me although I had told her neither my mission nor destination.

This time I noticed Christmas decorations, swags of tinsel and frosting everywhere, and there came the sound of a carol, broken off at some childish disagreement. Santa stood in full finery at the end of the central passageway and a very small girl was reaching up to place a very large note in the North Pole Post Office Box beside him. The nun stopped to assist.

"Do you think he'll get it all right?" the child asked anxiously.

"Oh, I'm sure he will, Lynette," the nun answered soothingly, and with a last suspicious look to see that the letter had really dropped down the hatch the little girl ran away, at full tilt.

"I'm so glad you're going to see Laura, Doctor," said the

nun as we turned another corner. "We pray for her recovery every day."

"How did you know it was Laura I'm seeing, Sister?" I asked in surprise. But she merely smiled at my question. I was rapidly becoming accustomed to the fact that the nuns rarely spoke unless there was something definite to contribute. My question was shelved as a rhetorical one; that there was some intraspecific communication system afoot here, as reliable as that North Pole mailbox, I had already sensed.

"I hope this will be all right for you, Doctor," she said shyly, as she ushered me into a room that was apparently to serve as my office. "If there's anything you'd be wanting . . ."

"Thank you, Sister, this'll be fine."

"Laura will be down right away." She smiled and left me.

I hung my coat and hat on the steel stanchion behind the door. It was a clean, spacious, but comfortless place with a desk, a telephone, and closets; it faced out onto an endlessly long corridor. I lit a cigarette and began my wait for Laura.

I did so, I must admit, more and more uneasily. Had I bitten off more than I could chew? What would happen if I failed? Why hadn't I picked on any one of the other girls who also needed help, and had more hope of recovery? I tried to relax as I remembered a tag from some poem I'd read:

There will be time, there will be time
To prepare a face to meet the faces that you meet . . .

As I waited I realized what a time it must have taken to decorate the long hallway, for it was festooned with paper-chains, hung with colored lanterns, the like. Someone, between 5 A.M. and midnight, had pasted paper decals of holly to each individual windowpane and sprayed their achingly high surfaces with messages in white frosting. MERRY XMAS was there in many languages, JOYEUX NOEL . . . FELICES NOVEDADES.

Language

I heard the sound of steps at the far end of the hall and leaned forward in my chair. Two figures came into view. Led by a nun, Laura was walking toward my office. There was no turning back now. I had committed myself.

In fact, the word "walking" can scarcely be used to describe that painfully laborious process. The girl had her head bent forward, while her body leaned for support against the gaily decorated wall at almost every step. Now and then, strolling patiently beside her, the nun would extend a steadying hand under her arm, or around her poor, curved back. As I watched, I realized what a miracle indeed is man; the muscular adjustments of balancing we make in walking are so taken for granted, they are so intrinsically human—like speech—that only their failure attracts attention. I had their failure before me now, as the sister, with a smile, helped the girl into a chair beside my desk.

"Laura, this is the doctor I told you about. He wants to talk with you a little."

"Hello, Laura," I said.

"Call me when you want me, Doctor," said the nun. "I'll be right down." Before leaving she gave me a sympathetic shake of her head behind the girl's back.

"Hello, Laura," I tried again, softly.

She sat doubled in the chair, head drooping, motionless, her dark blond hair straggly and strawlike. Her clothes were clean, the navy skirt worn by those of her age group in the Institution well pressed, but her blouse, I noticed, was incorrectly buttoned. She wore thick glasses and I could see that her eyes were severely crossed. The left side of her face was badly scarred, the skin almost purplish in places. Her legs, in their neat tan nylons, were badly marred by protruding veins.

She said nothing. She did not move. Only her right hand rose, very slowly and deliberately, so that for a moment I wondered what she was going to do. Her nose was running, and slowly she wiped off the drip with the back of her hand, and then lowered her hand to her lap.

During that entire first interview, or meeting, in fact, I became mesmerized by the regularly increasing drip from Laura's nostrils. Would she wipe it off? Would she not wipe it off? Sometimes she did, and sometimes she didn't. But at that time I was clinging to straws and I tried to tell myself that, each time she did so, it was a sign of self-respect, and human dignity. For this was very much worse than I'd expected. Despite all my reading of the case I knew there was a lot more to be learned, and a long, long way to go.

"It'll be Christmas soon, Laura. I like Christmas, don't you?"

It is an unnerving experience to find oneself face to face with another human being who is alive, but not really living, who can feel but is not really feeling, who can think but is not really thinking. In those first moments between us the silence was deafening. It seemed something tangible, embracing the room, flowing out into the hallway and swelling through the entire Institution—something I had to conquer. And in that spirit I reasoned that, if Laura couldn't talk to me, I would at least talk to her.

So I began a monologue that was to be one of hundreds. I have always believed that language is our greatest gift for human co-operation and common understanding; and I have always been drawn to those linguists who have found it a uniquely human quality. No tribe, however primitive, has ever been found without language. Not only is every human experience saturated with verbalism—a child loves flowers increasingly as it masters their names—but words also discover meaning for us, they help us to survive. This deep form of human communication was lost to the bowed figure in front of me.

My monologue was, indeed, an object lesson in the "gift of tongues." Since Laura made not the slightest reaction, I had no guidelines to follow in what I said. I was verbally blind. I might as well have talked nonsense—and I am not sure that at some points I didn't.

Why, I was not even certain she could hear me. No, there stretched a long path through a lot of darkness ahead and as I stumbled along it in those early steps, trying to think of something to say to this "human vegetable," I fortified myself with memories of how deprived and mistreated she had been; I buoyed myself up by trying to bear in mind that she was really only an infant of six months of age, who had had to suffer constant hurt. I remembered Jack Di Salvio, and that pink stone building. Even so, I know I flagged. The task of tempting this hidden spirit out of her isolation seemed veritably monumental. At times I think I panted aloud.

"Listen, Laura," I said as gently as I knew how, "we're going to meet twice a week. Maybe we'll play or talk or just sit here together."

Her head remained lowered, her body unnaturally rigid. Signs of life were barely perceptible. After less than an hour I rang for the nun, who came and tenderly escorted Laura on the long trek back to her room.

Oddly enough, when her presence had left me, my office seemed strangely empty, although she had not said a word. With my thoughts racing, I lit another cigarette and walked to the window giving onto the street. One or two stores, a rundown grocery. Someone had scrawled on a wall, Johnny U + Edna. Someone else, The Unknown Mike. This time the bus I saw had emblazoned on its cheerful flank OH, TO BE YOUNG AND IN NEW YORK/ AND HAVE RESERVE MONEY IN THE BANK/ PRIVILEGE CHECKING. . . . I should have to be patient, as patient as the nuns, with this small morsel of humanity.

Instead of writing notes, as is my custom after such an interview, I sat in the stillness that Laura had left and tried to think. I looked around the room and realized that it was too big for a very little girl to bear. Its proportions would make her feel insignificant, frightened. Secondly, there was insufficient stimulation, not enough objects to catch her eye and give me a chance to start communicating with her in some way. I turned to my phone and called the superintendent. Her resonant voice came back at once.

I explained that I needed a smaller room, one more pleasantly decorated, and, if possible, filled with certain kinds of toys. She replied graciously and I reeled off a list of items I had been jotting on the pad before me. I wanted clay and finger paints, puppets, paper, crayons, blocks, little dolls, and a doll house.

I added, "If possible, also a nurse doll, a doctor doll, a miniature stethoscope, and tiny rolls of bandages."

"Yes, Doctor, I quite understand. We will get them for you."

I paused. "By the way, I'll need to talk with her group mother."

"It has already been arranged."

This time my pause was even longer.

"Are you there, Doctor?"

"I think I would also meet some more of those who work directly with the children, Sister."

"At any time," came the voice. We rang off.

I stood up, feeling oddly exhausted. I am not usually talkative, and my monologue had taken more out of me than I cared to acknowledge. Usually in such interviews I listen.

But now that I had met Laura I wanted to meet, too, the only family she had ever known, the nuns who looked after her and the children among whom she lived. The Institution was her family. This, I said to myself, is where she is, at least, accepted; this is where she lives. So far her life had had three partitions to it: a short and agonizing year and a half with her parents, followed by three and a half years in the hospital and shelter, and then seven years here at the Institution. Of the three, this was as close to any home as Laura was presently likely to get.

I also wanted to know everything about her parents. All the history contained was a few statistics, bare facts about their age, familial composition, and the usual fragments of information that form part of every clinical record.

Why did they try to kill their only child? The answer, confronting me on every page, was in that never-ending series of push-button labels—"psychotic," "alcoholic," "perverted" —by which society excuses itself to society, separating in neat compartments the "good guys" from the "bad guys," the so-called sick from the so-called well. I had to learn more about these people. I called Dorothy at the control office.

"I want to locate Laura's parents," I said.

She answered that she'd check the records at once and a little while later came back to tell me they were both currently in a local mental hospital—the husband's third admission in the past ten years.

"Let's see," she said, reminding me of some librarian checking on a book, "you'll find Mr. Meyer in C Building, Haltzer Unit, Ward 14. Mrs. Meyer's in A Building, Griffen Unit, Ward 16."

I thanked Dorothy, put the scribbled information in a side pocket, grabbed my coat, and headed home. It had indeed been a busy day.

5

The next morning I called my secretary and told her to push my appointments into the latter half of the day. I wanted to see Laura's parents.

A half hour later I found myself confronted by a city within a city. Stretching for three blocks or more, there lurked another faceless structure, and if this gray hulk boasted no barbed wire on its walls, it had iron bars on each window and at the top a roofed exercise area heavy with grilling.

Inside I was directed through littered halls and drab passages. The lighting was poor, the paint peeling, the walls cracked. Listless groups congregated here, or shuffled aimlessly in slippers—some of them white, some black, some yellow, some gray. These forgotten and disheveled corpses, staring through empty hours, mumbled occasionally as I went by, but otherwise gave small signs of life, leaning on walls, tagged and embalmed, if not yet buried.

C Building, Haltzer, was for males only. Dr. Crager, a short, stocky man in his forties, met my request with polite puzzlement. Rubbing his forehead, he guessed vaguely, "Must be new here. We have about two hundred patients to each doctor. They come and go, it's tough to keep track of them all. Let's see. Isn't Meyer the chubby fellow with the . . . ah no, that's Simpson. Let me get his chart out for you. This man has to be new."

The record-room clerk produced Martin Meyer's case history. The size of the file made it apparent that he was far from a newcomer to the hospital.

Dr. Crager glanced over the record briefly. "Third time around in ten years. Not bad. So far this admission seems to have been for about four months. Paranoid schizophrenic, complicated by chronic alcoholism." He rattled off the terms in vigorous summary and shook his head with a smile. "Interesting fellow. We also have his wife in the Griffen Unit. Strange couple. Can't live together, yet can't seem to live apart. I'll arrange for you to meet him right away."

He led me back through the dismal, tissue-strewn hallways into a small cell containing a broken bed and a wooden chair.

"Sorry I don't have anything better at the moment, but if you want to be alone . . ."

"This'll do," I said. "Thanks."

Dr. Crager left me with a nod. I took off my coat and looked for a hook. There were none. I put it on the faded bed. The room was bare, in the sense of being conspicuously void of all protrusions. There were no hooks on which to hang a coat, or hang a man. The single dusty bulb was flush with the ceiling and heavily caged. No patient could end his misery here by self-electrocution. I pulled the chair up under the barred window and began to read:

Martin Meyer, 51, oldest of five (Evelyn, Sandra, Phyllis, Paul) . . .

So the record opened. It was apparently an immigrant family, whose father had operated a fruit store over which they had lived in a three-room apartment. It was an easy enough picture to reconstruct: one sink, a closet toilet with hanging chain, worn linoleum, a ceiling made of stamped-out tin, one dangling, furry lightbulb, and a washing line strung from the pipe of a stove, which featured repeatedly in the notes taken later from Martin's tapes.

The boy had slept with his sister Evelyn, three years his junior, and according to his parents was a quiet, emotion-

less child, "a good kid" who would one day be "somebody."
Too busy to make neighborhood friends, and, in those few
moments his father allowed him from the store, he preferred
to play with his toy soldiers rather than roughhouse with
the others. He was, in a word, "different." The word indeed
figured frequently in the dossier I held in my hands. "Prefers
to be alone . . . likes to be by himself. . . ."

The mother, Mrs. Meyer, had been a sickly woman, it
seemed, though from the written record it was hard to tell
just how sick she had really been or if she simply used her
sickness to control her children. (I guessed the latter to be
the case, as I read on.) Martin had been sympathetic to her
and she had thrived on his love, taking advantage of it to
send him on errands, get him to sweep up the store, and
the like. Up to this point there was nothing too unusual
in the record; Laura's father seemed to have spent his boyhood days helping his parents, huddling near the big stove,
and playing with his lead soldiers. Then, as I turned the
page, I came to the crisis of his youth, one that had turned
it into that nightmare of half-understood guilt which eventually had rebounded on his own daughter.

Evelyn, the beauty of the family, a slender girl with long
black hair, had been Martin Meyer's boyhood love. Martin
had told the doctors in detail how he had loved to brush
the great black mass of her hair. His sister would often
insist that he stroke harder, until the jolts disturbed her back.
At night Martin would lie awake and crush the lustrous
stuff in his fingers, careful not to awaken his sister. Then
a few days before his fifteenth birthday Evelyn was rushed
to the hospital, dying of polio. The household became an
agony of whisperings, of the mother's tears and the father's
groans. It was clear that whatever secret death wishes, born
of envy, Matin had nurtured for his beloved sister suddenly
threatened to turn into reality. The suppressed disgust he
had felt at himself, lying beside her and caressing her hair

while she slept, mounted to a climax. He was on the verge
of being victor and victim at the same time.

Evelyn came back to the house alive but in a squeaking
wheelchair, paralyzed from the waist down. For Martin it was
a day he would never forget, a day that haunted him. For
months he remained "depressed," probably in a stupor of
fear and guilt at the sight of his immobilized sister. The
newly crippled individual is thrown into the position of having
to accept definitions of his or her situation from without,
from other people. Martin was not capable of helping Evelyn
in this way, in her search for another self. The boy turned
more and more to his mother, and the more he turned to
her the more, obviously enough, she involved him in the
care of his sister. It was a vicious circle, indeed. He could
see now, in his hospital discussions, something of this growing
enslavement to the two women in his life, but at the time
there had been no escape. He had had legs. Evelyn had had
none. He could walk and run. She was helpless and seemed
increasingly determined to reduce him to a state of equal
helplessness. She began to learn to command. Evidently a
crude signal system was set up. Three slaps with an old
shoe on the linoleum floor meant that Martin had to come
up from the fruit store—running. Finally, goaded, there had
come the day when the boy had lashed back, hurting himself
by hurting her—"You're nothing but a cripple. You'll *never*
find a man now," he remembered having shouted at her;
then—"You might as well cut all your hair off and leave
it short. Forever."

I could see the scene, as gradually it had been drawn out
of Martin in his talks with the Doctors: the sickly mother
storming after the boy, her face full of fury; then whipping
him about the head and finally making him apologize to his sister *on his knees*. This had been insisted on, it seemed. Evelyn
hated him, he felt. His mother hated him. He rubbed and
cleaned his lead soldiers until they were shiny and bright.

But there was no place to be safe. . . . Then had come his revenge.

He had been ordered to take Evelyn out, out into the crisp spring air where children skipped rope and jumped and drew hopscotch courts on the sidewalk. He had wheeled her to the edge of the staircase, it seemed, and let her chair tremble there, closer and closer until he had been quite sure Evelyn was thoroughly frightened ("enjoyed seeing her fear," ran the notation). The girl had begun screaming, and the sight of her fear had sent a significant spider of excitement crawling up his spine. Evelyn had to beg, to beg and plead, and slowly Martin pushed the wheelchair ever closer to the edge. And at last she had begged, whimpering. Only then did he pull the chair back, out of danger.

The years sped by. There wasn't much on the boy's education. At seventeen he left school to work full time in the store, as well as, of course, answer (at once) the insistent banging of the slipper on the ceiling overhead.

Paradoxically, Evelyn's beauty increased. She was surrounded by gifts. In particular, mention was made of her love of peanut brittle. Martin's own eighteenth birthday stayed in his mind as marked by the contemptuously small cake bought from a bakery at reduced rate since it was over a day old. Both mother and sister clearly grew more and more skillful in making the big youth feel guilty or selfish.

A big youth he appeared to remain. There was little in the file, barring the blank of utter futility, between this date and Martin's thirtieth birthday. Here once more the marker was a red brand of agony on an already hypersensitized unconscious. Martin was to be thrown out of his home, disowned by his parents.

The record was elliptical, but, piecing it together, I could get the general gist. It was not so unusual a story. Martin had become a mere instrument of convenience, played on by the commands of ailing mother and crippled sister. Evelyn's insults evidently grew more provocative as Martin aged. Naturally enough, his own state of anxious helplessness infuriated him. He knew himself to be trapped by his feelings and the irony that, after enslavement to mother and sister, he was now a prisoner within himself.

Externally, his life was uneventful enough. His father accorded him a small salary. Martin worked long hours, going to the market at five every morning, unpacking fruit and vegetables, cleaning and sweeping, trying (he even confessed) to tire out his body so that his mind might be at peace. Then came the day when the girl, his own sister, struck at his manhood.

The Meyers, it seemed, seldom went out or socialized. They had little money to entertain or be entertained. But the evening of their thirty-first wedding anniversary had seemed a special occasion and accordingly Mr. Meyer arranged to take his wife to a local restaurant. Martin would be home as usual and could be depended upon to take care of Evelyn; the other children were now old enough to fend for themselves. It was a crisis point in an already unsteady life.

After the Meyers had gone out that evening, Martin sat staring at Evelyn. Soon he was to prepare her supper and afterward to clean the kitchen. But for a while he had just stared. And Evelyn had begun to feel frightened. To compensate, she began to needle him, as, with his back to her, he started on the task of breaking up some wooden boxes in his huge hands, stacking the planks next to the roaring stove.

"Say something, can't you?" she had cried at him then. "Speak to me. *Speak.* Why can't you speak?"

So it must have continued, while Martin stacked and broke the kindling, watching the greedy flames each time he raised the stove's ruddy lid.

"*Say something.* How come you don't go out with girls, I mean, Martin? Huh? There must be some girls, somewhere, that would find even *you* interesting." The gibes and jeers, and jeers and gibes, had gradually piled up like the planks from the broken fruit boxes—which the big hands tore into more and more rapidly. Martin admitted in analytic session that he knew he was losing control. Some crisis was upon him.

"Don't you like girls? Is that it? You ever kiss a girl, Martin? Properly, I mean. I'll bet you never."

He had slid past her into his room but there was no fleeing the softly mocking laughter that followed him, nor the taunts.

"How 'bout boys?" had cooed the disembodied voice behind him now; and Martin had tried not to hear. "Yeah. You like boys maybe?" And then it had come, explicitly. "Martin. You listening? What's a queer?" His hands had started moving; he tried to sit on them on the bed, but they had crept out from under him "like live things." He had watched them move. Out of control. And the all-knowing voice of the woman he admired most in life had flicked at him like a whiplash—"You a queer, Martin?"

Out of control, Martin clearly had been terrified. He had heard music, so he had told one doctor, had seen flashing images of his mother, memories of childhood, open flames leaping out at him, and to another physician he had recalled at this moment seeing himself falling off a tall building, turning over and over, to hear the final thud of his body thumping the sidewalk. Actually, he had hurled himself at his sister and grabbed her, thrusting her out of the wheel-chair and onto the bed. His hands had tightened "as though of themselves" around her neck, and he had tried to strangle her.

Some moment, or eternity, later Martin had felt himself thrown to the floor. His father was leaning over him, beating him about the face. His mother sat holding his sobbing sister, while from her distracted lips came the words: "Get out of here, get out of here. Never come back. *Get out now.*" Martin Meyer never forgot those words.

He gathered his few belongings in an old shopping bag

and went into the street. That night he slept in the fruit store, which he entered through a poorly locked back window. The next day he was off roaming the streets.

I sat back for a second and thought about what I had read. I heard the shuffle of feet outside the door, and so absorbed had I been in these records that I almost imagined Martin himself there. But the dossier, when I returned to it, became skimpy, and necessarily disconnected. All the information about this part of his life that Martin had disclosed consisted, it seemed, in a succession of briefly held jobs. "Dishwasher . . . scrubman . . . grease monkey . . . laborer . . . telegram runner. . . ." He had even, for a time, been a panhandler on subways. Mostly, he became an expert at getting out of tenements before landlords caught up with him. The rent sharper par excellence. Finally, he found a job at O'Reilly's Bar and Grill.

Here he had worked washing dishes and helping with orders, getting to the bar whenever he could, for there had been free drinks in the pink-rose twilight of O'Reilly's Bar and Grill. Women and liquor and warmth. All three made Martin manly. He could be "someone," after all. And one evening a "client" had told him of "a certain little organization" badly in need of talent. Martin Meyer entered the business of lending money.

Here there seemed a turn upward in his fortunes. For the first time he was in a position of power—and women came into his life. There were many of these, but on the record they were mostly names. He obviously had had a knack for picking on very dependent and submissive women who looked up to him like some forgotten father. To him women were all helpless children, and if they obeyed blindly he was benevolent enough. But when they became possessive, he turned violently abusive. On collection night he was a martinet.

He was a winner and his nonpaying clients were losers. He became a primitive hostile being, devoid of all compassion.

51

At the height of his new-won glory he called up all his courage and paid a visit to his family. On the way he bought presents, including flowers for his mother and for his favorite sister a box of peanut brittle. It was a weird meeting in that already rebuilt neighborhood.

What I could gather from the history was that Martin had gone back, found the fruit store in its same place, and started on his way up that creaky stair where he had once balanced the pleading Evelyn between life and death. And, as if prearranged, as if out of some bad dream or second-rate soap opera, a woman with sunken cheeks and a black shawl drawn around her shoulders had been standing there.

"Mother!" he had cried. "How are you, Mom? Gee, you look . . . great."

But as he began to stagger up the first steps toward her, he froze. The frail figure, clad entirely in black, said nothing. Only the intensity of her grip on the handrail had altered. He had questioned her again, spilling his parcels, holding out the flowers, his mouth moving ominously as her silence persisted.

"What do you expect? Want me to get down on my hands and knees or something?"

His voice had risen. His nostrils had started to twitch. Only after a long pause did the specter speak.

"My son Martin," it said in a calm, empty tone, "died some time ago. He left our home. We mourned him a week."

But he was alive, Martin had protested, here he was, her own son, standing right there before her, and, what's more, entitled to a bit of respect.

"Martin is dead and buried. Martin is in hell."

The eyes had gazed over or beyond or through him, until he had in desperation and growing fear stumbled up the steps to her, holding out the peanut brittle.

"Look. Mom. I have money now. Position. I brought something special for Evelyn, I know she'll like it, it was always her favorite. . . ."

But like an old phonograph with its needle stuck, the voice had gone on again, "Evelyn is dead. Martin, our son, killed Evelyn."

He had started back at that, eyes aghast. His bushy hair began to sprout sweat.

"She died of a broken heart three weeks after Martin left our home."

That was what Martin Meyer reported his mother as having said, in that extraordinary confrontation, not only with his past but with all the hidden fears of his unconscious. He had protested again but his mother had turned away. Above and beyond him Martin heard her saying, "Evelyn is dead. You killed her a million times, Martin. You are an animal. Get out of this house and never come back."

What happened next was vague, even to Martin. It was hard to sort out, at least on the printed page, what was reality and what was fantasy, what he had done and what he dreamed he had done.

At least he seemed to have walked the streets in a throbbing daze, until it was dark and lights streamed on the rain-soaked avenues. It had been raining hard, he had recounted on one occasion, but he himself had felt nothing. There had been a throbbing pain in his head, compounded with hooting cars, the rumbling of the el, the blaring sounds from bars. Sweat stood on his brow, his hands crawled, his pace increased. Occasionally he would break into a run, glancing back over his shoulder at the voices that called out his name.

"I wasn't afraid," he kept reassuring the Doctor. "There was no one there."

A subway entrance seemed inviting. He jumped in the first train, sat down, loosened his collar, and stared at the people around him. They seemed angry at him for something. Why? He had to keep calm. "What did you say?" he would ask now and then, as the train pulled up at a stop. "How's that? Speak up."

They were whispering. He couldn't stand it any longer, got out of the subway car, ran up the staircase, through the streets, and up the long flights to his own room, where he threw himself on the bed. He had to be calm, he had to hide. He was trembling all over.

As the hours passed he lay there pinpointing every sound in the room with manic concentration. Finally there had come one that was a little different. A cat mewed outside his door. He opened the door and took it into his room and stroked the soft fur, and even, it seemed, offered it the peanut brittle, which it declined.

He lay there with the cat cupped in his huge hands, but the headache was getting worse, and the voices were starting again, accumulating finally to a chaotic clamor of accusatory sirens. He writhed on the bed, crying, "Stop it! Please, please. Please stop it, I tell you."

The alarmed cat had struggled in his grip, and he had had to squeeze very hard, at the soft fur of the neck, until the limp velvet lump fell to the floor and Martin Meyer faced the voices, rushing into the hallway, yelling and screaming, "I killed her . . . I killed my sister . . . *leave me alone!*"

The record showed that one Martin Meyer, aged thirty-eight, was admitted to a mental hospital at 2 A.M. that cold October morning. He had been lightly clad, and kept on babbling something about peanut brittle.

There he remained for over six months. His hallucinoses were as long and monotonous as the days of depression on the hospital cot. Doctors would ask him about the voices and he would simply shake his heavy head. Were they real? Were they false?

Then for the first time they wheeled him, horizontal, to the treatment room. He had described this first initiation into our electrical Tartarus in grim detail. There was three nurses, plus a husky Negro attendant who had kept wiping sweat off Martin's brow as the wheels beneath made a soft, contused sound on the cheap tiling.

"Just take it easy, boy. I won't let them hurt you. Don't fight it now, and you won't feel a thing."

Caged lights passed in a steady rote overhead, and the mumbling by his side reminded him of people praying. Then the cortege of four stopped and looked down at him with mournful expressions, as if to say farewell. The big man stirred uneasily.

At which point the bodies about him stiffened like puppets, as suddenly they pressed hard to hold him down.

Expertly, one nurse plugged his mouth with a red rubber tube, another adjusted the dials on a gleaming machine leaking wires toward him. The third pasted his temples for the electrodes.

"Don't fight it, boy. You're going to be fine now. Just wait."

The rubber strap was cold on Martin Meyer's forehead, and when he opened his eyes, many hours later, his tongue felt twice its size, he had a splitting headache, and the Negro male nurse at his side was smiling.

"Now what I tell you, boy?"

The series of shock treatments that ensued seemed to change very little. The entry of that long table on wheels soon made Martin dissolve into frantic hysteria.

Three months later he was finally discharged, a wounded, muddled man, with a strange sense of detachment and very little confidence left in his saggy bulk at all.

What did Martin do? The record was by no means always clear. Trucker's help, ironworker, derrick operator, factory laborer, odd-job man, truck driver's assistant—the employment was usually in conformity with his size. But this was far from the Martin who had made the world kneel at his feet. Once more the money lender's domination lured him. Here he was always on top. A winner to the core.

What he earned went on alcohol. Scotch became his courage, and his king. His thoughts were confused. Drinking seemed to help as it loosened his feelings and cleared his head from the long stream of obsessions and petty, repetitive ruminations that had of late intruded into his mind.

Getting back to the life he had started away from his own family was not easy after his stay in the hospital, but gradually with the help of alcohol Martin regained some of his courage. Whiskey became his tranquilizer and Martin needed more of it each passing week. Its effect on him was astonishing. It loosened his tongue, deepened his voice, gave him stability. He gradually went from drinking in the evening to beginning each day with a few just to steady his nerves. Then this was followed by a few at lunch, and before long each drink was separated by only an hour.

Martin's capacity to tolerate liquor increased with time, and the fact that he began to put on weight gave him an even greater tolerance. He enjoyed the feeling of friendliness and proximity to people at the various bars where he drank. He could now put his arms around men he met telling them of his difficult life, while at the same time reeling off his many exploits with women, most of them figments of his imagination.

In his loan work, and through the power of money, it was not difficult for Martin to find women whom he could sexually master while at the same time remaining emotionally detached from them. It was a man's world, in Martin's terms, and women had their place. He also enjoyed spending his time with men in bars, at dinner, or in business dealings. Slowly his group of male friends increased and he was given recognition by them. He had become outspoken, sometimes daring, and his facility for being the center of attention, joking, drinking, and telling stories, gave him a status he had never enjoyed before. In the midst of the most serious conversation, Martin could easily be distracted by a good-looking female body that passed him. His detailed description of his love affairs fired the imagination of those around and served further to inflame his own desires.

He was in just such a mood when he met Adeline. She was alone and buying a drink at a bar Martin frequented. He was immediately drawn to her soft skin and long black hair. He stared at her for almost an hour while he fortified himself with whiskey. There was a soft, feminine glow about her, a tenderness he had not seen in any of the women he had been with before. He imagined her to be a "lady," in her thirties, and yet the fact that she was sitting in the bar alone disturbed his fantasies about her, because, after all, no decent girl would be found in a place like that.

He sat next to her, and as he began making his approach he could hear himself playing it "straight." He was polite, friendly, yet serious in his conversation, and she equally serious but friendly. He liked her. His mind quickly obliterated any of the doubts he had had about her respectability as he invited her to have dinner with him. The conversation continued to be congenial and Martin sensed his growing affection for Adeline like some shy adolescent who awkwardly tries to be nice to a girl he likes and respects. This was a new feeling for Martin and he called it love.

They saw each other frequently after that night and he liked what he felt about her. She was a sensitive, helpless creature of beauty who had also come from a disrupted home life. Her mother had died when Adeline was two and she had grown up as the mother of the house, taking care of the other four children and her father. When she was ten, her father remarried, to a woman much younger, and Adeline and her stepmother never got along. Adeline respected her, however, and continued to be devoted to her father, while her stepmother did as little as possible in the actual care of the house. Her father died when Adeline was sixteen, and life at home became unbearable.

These biographical details about Laura's mother, thirty-five years old when Martin met her, came through fragmentarily in the record I was reading, and in greater detail from the woman's own file, which I perused later. I write them here to give continuity to Laura's story.

The two, in any case, had a lot in common, as Dr. Crager had correctly hinted. The same cycle of dependency and anger was there, the reciprocal needs of submission and domination. Here was a lamb, Martin had thought, and he had been willing enough to prove his love for Adeline by marrying her. So three weeks later a justice of the peace had officiated at this most holy alliance, whose celebration lasted two full days as Martin and his bride drank themselves into a series of stupors. The clutter of whiskey bottles, and half-eaten sandwiches, and empty coffee containers was the ceaseless backdrop of their married life. On the day when Adeline told her husband they were going to have a baby, Martin had raised his drink-befuddled head, squinted at his spouse, and said straight out, "Get rid of it."

Another time he had said, "Look. I'll buy you a coat instead. You'd like a nice warm fur coat, wouldn't you, sweetheart?"

But, in spite of his talk about buying a fur coat, life for Martin Meyer became even tougher. He was apparently—so I read between the lines—pushing hard on his clients to pay their debts. At the same time, he was frightening a lot of prospective customers off. He lost his "concession," as he liked to call it, and his references preceded him in other areas. With no money, a pregnant wife, and a cell for home, he was once more bitter, and scared inside.

Adeline, it seemed, largely stayed in her room in a general pattern of sleep and drink. Indeed, Martin's anxieties drove her deeper into this release, which rapidly reached the proportions of insensibility. The couple cried and fought, and more than once Adeline was given a beating "for her own good."

In his cups Martin would shout at her, "I'm your son . . .

I'm alive . . . don't call me an animal . . . I'm Martin your son."

"Crawl, Martin, crawl. Look at my own strong man, crying like a baby. Who's afraid now? Let me see you crawl while I spit in your face. Come to mamma, come."

That was the time he had smashed the nearest bottle on the bedpost and, with its jagged edges glittering, advanced toward her. Secure in the sight of his first tears, she had stood in defiance of his threat.

"Go ahead, Martin, why don't you kill me?"

"I never killed Evelyn. . . . Who said I killed her? Only a cat I killed. I squeezed its goddamn neck."

He had babbled on, and the moment of menace had passed in another alcoholic debauch. Finally, he left her one morning and didn't return.

As soon as she could think straight it was clear to Adeline that Martin had abandoned her. Her lifelong dread was upon her. She was alone and lonely, and about to give birth. She began going over to the local bar in the evenings, to "take the edge off" her loneliness. Occasionally she picked up some drunk who hadn't managed to see her protruding stomach but had been drawn to her pale face and long black hair, and went home with him. Staggering home one evening alone she collapsed on the street and was rushed, drunk, to the emergency room of a nearby hospital to give birth to a little girl with the first flecks of golden hair. It had been a nurse who had suggested she call her child Laura.

The infant was a year old when Martin chose to return home. Now there were three in the cell, a more cynical Adeline, Martin the morose, and the golden-headed baby. The mother tried to bring the two together without success.

Martin was unable to come to terms with the child.

He never once touched her. He confessed that he had to force himself to walk past her outstretched arms with averted face, and eyes squeezed shut. "I don't know what got into me," he said. "But she cried too much."

The baby's crying seemed to him to increase the ferocity of his headaches.

"Kids are like anyone else," he had once complained to Adeline. "Unless you're careful they'll be walking all over you."

The baby screaming. Headaches. Complaints from the neighbors. The Meyers had had to move. Through a barfly friend they heard of the flat above the pastry shop run by the Di Salvios. One afternoon they moved in with a few sticks of furniture, a supply of liquor, and one baby girl. It wasn't long before Florence Bernstein had been complaining too.

"When that shitbrat cries," Martin Meyer would moan, holding his heavy head in calloused hands, "it's like this goddamn needle going through my head. I tell you, I can't stand it. These headaches. Nobody seems to give a damn about *me*."

Perhaps it was some agonizing recollection of his own cry unheard, the deafening angry reminder of his dead sister. Whatever it was, Laura became his own inner suffering. And so one evening he decided to put an end to this embodiment of everything he hated in himself, and others. That was the night he put Laura in a frying pan and turned on the flame.

At this point, I recall, someone screamed in a distant passageway. I heard attendants running. Slowly I closed the case folder and relaxed for a minute, staring out the barred window onto a sky like blotting paper. I thought of all the Martin and Adeline Meyers there were in our cities, and of that thin line which separates their misery from our so-called normality. The scapegoats can take various forms—racial, religious, national hatreds of one kind or another.

I glanced at my watch and saw I would have to hurry. The reading had taken up more time than I'd expected. I checked once more in the record; it showed that Martin Meyer had been admitted to the mental hospital the very night he had tried to kill Laura. The official diagnosis was schizophrenic reaction, paranoid type.

The American Psychiatric Association classification manual defines a diagnosis of this kind as follows:

> This type of reaction is characterized by autistic, unrealistic thinking, with mental content composed chiefly of delusions of persecution and/or grandeur, ideas of reference and often hallucinations. It is often characterized by unpredictable behavior, with a fairly constant attitude of hostility and aggression. . . . There may be an expansive delusional system of omnipotence, genius or special ability.

In Martin's case the hospital doctors had further indicated, "Prognosis—guarded." This referred to the possibility of improvement, for in this disorder there is no "cure." By its size alone this human disaster, its treatment and prevention, remains one of the major human challenges of our time.

During this second admission Martin was given another series of electro-convulsive treatments, better known as shock therapy. Though frankly delusional for many months, he quieted to almost a model patient. Such remissions are not unusual when the psychosis subsides.

His secondary symptoms and ideas of reference disappeared and he took part fruitfully in hospital therapy and recreational programs, at which point—after some three years in the hospital—his diagnosis was changed to schizophrenic reaction, residual type. In his fourth year he was considered fit to be discharged into the community, remaining on convalescent care as an outpatient of the mental health clinic. Finally, he was released altogether from technical supervision.

His third admission in the past decade of his life was the consequence of an attempt to **ch**oke his wife to death while in an alcoholic rage. He believed he had just walked out of a coffin into his apartment, where, once again, he confused his wife with his mother. Adeline had summoned the police.

Dr. Crager was at the door. "All through?" he asked, smiling. "I have him waiting now, and if you'd like to use my office . . ."

"Thanks a lot. That'd be fine. All this has been most helpful."

It had. It had also been deeply alarming. Martin Meyer still had legal right to the custody of his child.

"How long do you think he'll remain here in the hospital?" I asked Dr. Crager as we made our way through the dismal corridors.

"Well, we try not to keep them long. As soon as his symptoms are cleared up we'll have him ready for discharge and place him on an outpatient basis."

"Mightn't that be rather dangerous?"

"Well, we can't keep him here forever. He'll recover much more quickly if we can get him back to work, and general life in the community."

"He has a daughter, you know," I interrupted. The man beside me nodded amicably. "He once tried to kill her, didn't he?"

Dr. Crager shrugged. "Who knows where she is now? We'll have to jump that hurdle when we come to it. Frankly, we don't believe in keeping our patients locked up indefinitely just because they *may* kill someone. After all," he concluded with a laugh, "if we did that, we'd have to lock up most of the world, wouldn't we? No, the percentage of potentially dangerous cases in the total of mentally ill is relatively small. In spite of what the general public may think, the overwhelming number of major crimes are not committed by the mentally sick."

"So you don't consider Martin Meyer a menace?"

Dr. Crager gave my shoulder an avuncular pat as we rounded a last corner. "Let's just say unpredictable, shall we. Paranoids are. Right now he's getting on well. But, here's my office and if you'd wait in here I'll bring him to you."

Less than a minute later Laura's father was sitting in front of me. I felt I had known him all my life.

Physically he was as I'd pictured, a strongly built man of medium height in his early fifties, with heavy shoulders and curly, graying hair growing low over a craggy forehead, beneath which his pale eyes were set deep. They moved a lot. His nostrils, which were hairy, twitched energetically as he spoke.

"You going to handle my case now?" he asked with a suspicious blink as Dr. Crager left us.

"No," I answered, "I just wanted to talk with you about your family."

"Sure," he replied with surprised alacrity. "Dr. Crager tells me I should co-operate, and anything he says goes with me. What did you say your name was?"

I gave it.

"Nice name," he mused, grinning. "Just what kind of a doctor are you, Mac?"

"Psychoanalyst."

"Oh." A pause. His nostrils fidgeted briefly. "I always admire an educated man."

"Care for a cigarette, Martin?"

"Yeah, thanks. Like I say, I might have made a good doctor myself. I tell you, it hasn't been easy."

"I'm sure it hasn't," I said.

"Now we got to concentrate, see. Concentrate on the future. And *that* means I got to get well again. You don't appreciate that till you been sick. Develop respect for life." From under the craggy brows his eyes darted over me briefly. "Now, like there's an interesting word. Respect, I mean. All you educated guys are so full of respect, and . . . and . . . education. Well, I tell you I was respected, highly *respected* in my profession."

"You were a loan shark, weren't you, Martin?" I said,

choosing my words on purpose. I wanted to see how thin the façade was. Sure enough, it provoked the anticipated reaction.

"I didn't call you a shrink, did I?" He was angry. Then the smile took over, like the sun after some fleeting cloud. "I was in the business of loans, all right. I was no gangster."

"I'm sorry, Martin. I meant no offense."

"Yeah. I like that. Apologizing." He blew a stream of smoke into my face. "Makes you feel good, huh?"

"If you want to look at it that way."

"Well, a lot of guys respected me and still do. You ask my name in any of the bars Lower East Side, you'll find they know Martin Meyer right enough."

"Tell me about your family."

"That ain't hard. I have a lovely and devoted wife with beautiful . . . beautiful black hair, and a daughter who is living kinda with an aunt, while my wife and I get out and on our feet."

I said nothing for a moment.

"It's these headaches," he said.

"How old's your daughter?" I asked.

His brow furrowed further. "Must be about thirteen now. Thirteen, fourteen. Lovely girl with golden hair. The most lovely hair you ever saw. Gee, I'm crazy about Laura." The word hung in the air an instant. Then he laughed nervously. "Dr. Crager hear me say that, he'd lock me up and throw away the key, huh?"

"Your wife, Adeline?"

"Well now, she's had a rough time of it. Used to drink plenty, too. Y'know how it is. They said I tried to kill her. Must have been drunk to try that 'cause I do love that woman. I'm telling you, Doc, she's a creature of beauty, and refinement, and I love all beautiful things." Leaning forward in his seat, bunched, he stared straight at me. "I mean—do I look like the kind of guy who'd want to kill another? You're not . . . *afraid* of me, are you, Doc? Maybe I do drink too much, at that, lose my temper now and then. So okay. I didn't *kill* anyone in my life, did I?"

"I didn't say you killed anyone, Martin."

"No?" His nostrils twitched actively, his lips moved. He sat back as if exhausted. Then, with a smile stealing catlike over his features, he raised one stubby finger. "Doc, you sure are smart. Almost you trapped me there. Almost you made me confess. How d'you like that! But it didn't work, did it? Now you just go back and tell her it didn't work."

"Tell whom, Martin?"

The smile broadened, as if with complicity. "Two can play at that game, Doc. No one makes a monkey out of Martin Meyer."

After some more of the same, Dr. Crager stuck his head around the door and, at a nod from me, took Martin back to his ward. I thanked him as he did so and headed for the other side of the hospital to try to see Adeline.

There a Dr. Austin met me, a tall individual with thinning fair hair slicked back over his head. Though he had only been on the staff a few months, he seemed to know Adeline Meyer well, and conversed easily about her. This was evidently her second admission and she, too, had been "inside" some three months now. On admission she had been intoxicated, agitated, delusional, and hallucinatory.

Dr. Austin loaned me his office and said he would find Mrs. Meyer for me.

As I glanced through her record I found that it showed a diagnosis on first entry of schizophrenic reaction, paranoid type—exactly the same as that of her husband. On her second, her diagnosis was schizophrenic reaction, acute undifferentiated.

This was perhaps small wonder. Just prior to his attempt to kill her, Martin had knocked her unconscious with a bedroom chair. Adeline was shown in. The mother of Laura now stood before me. Her uncombed hair was partly gray. Her face was caught in powdery wrinkles, and she looked older than her alleged forty-seven years. She sat down and placed her hands in her lap, her head bent slightly forward.

She seemed to be making a big effort to follow everything I said. While we talked I tried to catch some similarity between her features and those of Laura. The resemblance was small but there. I told her I had just had her husband with me.

"Oh him." Her head came up. "You saw Martin? Is he well? I miss him, kinda. The poor dumb guy who was scared of ghosts."

"Ghosts?"

"Yeah. Can you believe that, Doctor? A little baby ghost drove my Martin crazy. Afraid of the dark. That great big son of a gun. Amazing. Cry like a baby at night and push men over bars in the daytime. See, the light used to keep Laura—that's my daughter—awake. How come someone can be as strong as that and as weak as a baby at one and the same time? Now you tell me that. Huh? Gee, you wouldn't know what I been through. Why, he even tried to *kill* me once. You know that? Just an animal. Then confusing me with other people. Hell, I wish I had a drink. My hair needs a wash. You don't have a smoke, do you, Doc? What a dump this is."

It all came spilling out.

"Treat you like animals here . . . I miss him, all the same . . . wants people to treat him like royalty, see, and then steps all over 'em when they do. Jesus, what a character."

"Why do you keep going back to him then, Adeline?" I interposed at one point.

Head on one side, she considered for a moment. "I guess because I'm lonely," she said at last, with a slow smile, close to a leer. "Makes me feel good when he wants me . . . even though he's so cruel . . . like that killing, killing. . . ." She ducked her head into her hands.

"Killing whom, Adeline?"

"My Laura, that's *who*," she cried hysterically. Her shoulders were shaking with sobs. "She was my baby, but he called her a screaming brat. He couldn't stand her from the minute she was born. She cried and cried, she was frightened, and I couldn't stand the noise, either . . . I tried to make her stop . . . then everything got confused, I don't know, and Martin was yelling at me to stop it, stop this goddamn noise, see, and the baby was crying all the time and my head began to burst. He lifted her by the arms and legs, and, and . . . oh I can't *talk* about it any more."

I let her cry distractedly for some minutes, then said softly, "Adeline. I have seen your daughter. She is alive and being taken care of."

Slowly the tear-smudged face rose from enfolded arms. "She is?" she said in a dazed way. "My Laura's alive? Oh God bless you, Doctor, God bless you. . . ."

I held up a hand. "I can't tell you where she is, Adeline. But I can tell you that we're doing everything we humanly can to help her."

Then the half-comprehending eyes turned suspicious also. "Why? Why should you want to help her? What does she look like? Is she pretty? No, she couldn't be. She must be all scarred from the burns. That bastard . . . you have to believe me . . . it was Martin wanted to kill her, to stop the crying, see . . . you *have* to believe me, Doctor. . . . I'm her mother, ain't I? I *loved* her. You must tell her that I always loved her. Promise," she wound up, with all the frantic, overwrought emphasis of which she seemed capable, "promise as you'll tell her, Doctor. I *know* my Laura loves me. You see," she added, speaking as if explaining some bizarre tongue to an idiot, "I—am—her—mother."

There was silence in the room, and silence in the hall outside. Somewhere, distant in the city, a siren lowed in an ascending spiral of sound.

"What does Laura say about me?" the woman before me all but screamed. "*You gotta tell me, Doctor!*"

No Language But a Cry

"Adeline, your daughter doesn't speak," I said, watching the face freeze in gradual understanding, the mouth open in a gaping O as what I'd said sank in. "She's a mute, Mrs. Meyer. She has never spoken a word."

6

The time arranged for me to meet with Laura's institutional "family" was right after my next interview with her. This took place after the holiday season and was as fruitless as the first; it left me, if anything, less hopeful. I sat waiting for the superintendent to call me up.

I knew the nuns belonged to a particular order dedicated to child caring; that some of them were teachers who went out and taught in the various parochial schools in the community; that others worked directly with the children in the Institution all the time, as group mothers each responsible for some twenty-five girls.

Under each group mother were two matrons and occasionally a lay counselor, who gave a hand with the kids. I was surprised to learn that almost all these women without exception tried to find some few seconds of their care-charged days to continue their own education leading to proficiency as teachers, child care nurses, or as social workers. I was beginning to develop some considerable trepidation about confronting a group of these intensely practical, as well as highly spiritual, women.

First of all, I had no experience in dealing with nuns. So far, my meetings with them had been mainly confined to the superintendent and the nun who answered the door. I was quite unsure of them as people and was not certain that when I met them as a group I would know how to act. I have never been an especially religious person and I didn't want to hurt their feelings; above all, I had no idea of their attitude toward analysis.

My phone trilled. "If you could come up to the main conference room, Doctor," said a gently compelling voice. "Do you know where that is?"

I answered affirmatively, and said that I'd be right up. I put away the case histories I was reading and began to walk down the long hall. Each time I did so now I was conscious of what a slow and painful journey it was for Laura.

As I went up the stairs this time, I thought back to when I'd been a child and to the many questions that occur to children regarding nuns—how they lived, what they did for fun, whether they ever joked with each other, how they put up with their strenuous routine, and why they became nuns in the first place.

When a child, I suppose I'd answered all these questions by denying the fact that they were people and assuming that they undoubtedly possessed some superhuman, or mystical, qualities. Now it was important for me to sense how the children living in the Institution perceived the nuns. Already I was certain that it was in quite a different way from that of my own experience as a child. It was growing clear to me that, far from being distant from them, many of these youngsters were emotionally involved with the nuns. Children desperately desire someone who can give to them unquestioningly, without counting the cost, or requiring anything in return.

So absorbed was I in these thoughts that I twice passed by the conference room door. When finally I entered the room I drew up short. I had been prepared to meet three or four nuns. Here, ranged about a lengthy, gleaming refectory table, were sixty!

The superintendent had summoned the entire community of sisters to meet me. And each and every one of them stood up together, with military precision, as I made my entrance.

I had no idea what to do. There was a vacant chair at one end of the table and, guided by a sister, I advanced hesitantly toward it. As soon as I reached it, another led the assembly in prayer. This reassured me somewhat since I felt that they obviously had a set procedure for this kind of meeting, and I decided to take my cue from them.

When the prayer had ended, with a fervent "Amen," I remained on my feet. After all, I could scarcely sit down first in the presence of sixty women! The nuns remained standing. The minute or so that passed while we faced each other, standing, seemed like an eternity. Finally, from the far end of the table, the superintendent smiled and in her most mellifluous voice said, "Wouldn't you be more comfortable sitting down, Doctor?"

I agreed gratefully. Once I was seated, the nuns, with a susurration of garments, followed suit. I began to understand that they were as unsure of themselves in front of me as I was in front of them. Each had a small white pad before her, for the purpose of taking notes, and stacked in the center of the table stood other pads. A small cardboard box contained neatly sharpened pencils. Instinctively, I lit a cigarette.

Almost at once I realized my gaffe. I looked wildly about the impeccable chamber and the more I saw of its shining surfaces and mirrorlike waxed floor the more I was convinced I was the first person ever to smoke there. I watched my ash grow with horror. The lit tip seemed to be fairly racing for my fingers, and I'd have to put it somewhere soon.

Then the sister on my immediate right, who had shown me to my chair, got up, made a sort of feathering motion with one arm, and, like a conjurer, produced from out of her voluminous sleeves a shining ashtray.

"We thought you might want to smoke, Doctor," she said with a smile, as she placed it triumphantly before me.

With a sigh of relief I laid my hot ash in the immaculate, no doubt especially procured, ashtray and waited for the superintendent to make the next move. She nodded and Sister

Paulette, in a very humble and warm manner, started by saying how grateful they all were that I had decided I could give a little of my time to a child at the Institution.

"You see, Doctor, our girls are not orphans, but rather children from broken homes. Their parents are mostly mentally ill or chronically disabled people who can't care properly for their offspring. And it's such a great injury for these children to be separated from their families at a time when they so need love. And thus," she went on in the same patient, somewhat stately tone, "many of them are bitter, and disillusioned, terribly upset and frightened. We love them and try to give them the very best we can for their physical, spiritual, and emotional needs. But every now and then a child has a problem so intense, and deeply rooted, that it will bite the hand that feeds it. They are very sensitive about being placed in an institution, you know, and feel terribly rejected and abnormal in comparison with children who live with their families. Yes," she said, lowering her eyes from mine, and shaking her head sadly, "it's a bitter pill they have to swallow coming here. They aren't able to understand all the problems involved. So some of them rebel, while others may give up the struggle altogether and withdraw into themselves, and become inaccessible. . . ." Her voice tailed off. "And then it's hard for us to reach them, you see."

How well I understood what she had been saying, and how profoundly, too, she had conveyed the nuns' deep concern for these abandoned children. Laura was a perfect example of what she had been describing—the institutionalized child.

I said, "I'm sure Laura is a case in point, Sister. She seems to me to have given up the struggle, just as you say."

A discussion proceeded, the nuns gradually expressing their feelings about their children. Listening to them one by one, I began to sense their inexhaustible love for their charges, together with—a corollary of this—their frustration over Laura. Unlike my childhood stereotypes, these nuns were far from aloof; on the contrary, one after another spoke enthusiastically about the problem of reaching Laura. Even those who spent many hours outside as teachers knew her and all at some time seemed to have tried to make some contact with her.

I slipped a second cigarette between my lips and, with another feathering motion, the sister at my side produced matches to light it with the same matter-of-fact legerdemain, from out of her elbows. They were talking quite openly to each other now and I listened to them avidly, anxious to pick up any hint about the girl I could. Looking from one to another, I saw that under their winglike wimples their faces were for the most part relatively young. Each seemed deeply interested in her particular group of children and needed no coaxing from me to tell of this incident or that concerning her family of girls. Soon the room was ringing with laughter, as one humorous anecdote after another was told.

Sister Paulette was of particular interest to me. She had been Laura's group mother for seven years and knew her best of all. As she talked, I watched her closely. She was a woman in her early forties, on the thin side, with an attractive, serious face, whose eyes seemed to draw under the shadow of her forehead in concentration whenever she spoke at length. Yet her expression was emphatic. She was very much a human being talking about another human being. Much of what she said I had read previously in the case history, but I wanted to catch anything that might add another piece to the puzzle of the girl who had begun life like some bad dream off the front page of *The Enquirer*.

Softly, and in a relaxed manner, she described how in these seven years she had taught Laura to take care of herself. When the child had first come to the Institution she had had to be dressed, and directed, like a baby. At first she had had no idea of cleanliness nor any desire for it. But little by little she had come to learn how to dress, take care of her clothes, keep her small possessions in orderly fashion, wash herself, and follow the simple routine of the place without difficulty.

"She had no visitors?" I asked.

"There was only the aunt, you see," responded Sister Paulette, leaning forward over the table, "and soon she vanished altogether. When I was still in touch with her at the beginning I invited her . . . I begged her . . . to come and see Laura, but she always seemed to have some excuse as to why she couldn't."

"Did the children in the group learn to live with her all right?"

"Ye-es, I think so. Of course, you know what children are." Sister Paulette's head bent, frowning in concentration. "On the whole they accepted her, and some of them tried to play games with her, while others made fun of her . . . called her names. She was always so frightened, and shy. I'm afraid she just spent most of her time staring out a window. . . . Oh, we tried so hard."

"She sometimes liked to knit," put in another nun.

"Yes, Sister Jeanne, you're right. I often found her knitting. She seemed to love that."

"You know, Doctor," said Sister Paulette, from the other end of the table, "now that you have agreed to help Laura I must tell you something else. I was fearful it might put you off. We try to have holidays here for the children, so that they can feel they have vacations like others. There are one or two volunteer families who will take a child with them to share their holiday. In the beginning Laura resisted this idea, then we became hopeful when she began to demonstrate some interest in it. But, well . . ." She broke off timidly, and glanced down at her wide, white nails.

"Go on, Sister," I prompted.

Sister Paulette looked up, as close to unhappy as I had seen her. "The only families we could get her to go to reported that Laura remained completely inaccessible and apathetic." She paused, eyes straining. "They never asked for her again."

For a minute there was silence in the room. To me it seemed like Laura's own silence, an admission of failure, something we all had to conquer. As if reading my thoughts, Sister Paulette continued:

"There is something I must tell you, Doctor, though of course it's only a hunch. Ever since she's been here Laura has never said a word, but yet I have always had the feeling she can speak. I'm sure she can. She does have language," said the thin nun positively, nodding till her headdress flapped. "She is simply withholding it from us."

"What basis do you have for this belief, Sister?" I asked.

"It's just that, well, even though Laura doesn't use words, I understand how she feels. I have always known when she's frightened, upset. She would come to me, you see, and sit on my lap in her crooked way, put her arms around my neck, hold tight and cry. I would never ask what it was that was terrifying her. It seemed pointless, perhaps even impolite. In the evenings I used to sit with her and read to her out of one of her favorite books. She likes short stories and occasionally, only very occasionally, something or other would bring a slight smile to her face, and I would thank God for that, and feel it to be a triumph. Oh yes, yes," the nun concluded, fixing me with burning eyes, "I am sure that Laura can talk."

"What in particular is she afraid of, Sister?" I inquired after a moment.

"Oh, apart from fire, heat, her great terror seems to be the night. I wasn't long discovering that. She'd only been here a short while when, in making my evening rounds of the dormitory, I discovered that she was the only child not asleep, but rather that she was crying, with head buried under her pillow and the blanket pulled up over her head also."

An infant crying in the night. It was exact. As I listened to Sister Paulette's sonorous and level tones, I knew there was not one of us in that room who was not deeply touched by what she said. For the nuns, in fact, it was more like a mortification, suggestive of some failure on their part. . . .

"So night after night I would find her hiding and crying to herself. I would sit with her through the dark hours holding her in my arms, rocking her. And it seemed to calm her a little, Doctor, because after I did this for a long while she'd become sleepy, and might even rest in sleep for the remainder of that night."

Which you came back and checked, I thought, before you got up at 5 A.M. and started your next exhausting nineteen-hour day.

"Then one night when I drew near her bed, I noticed a light underneath the cover, and when I raised the blanket I found Laura all crouched like a ball beneath the pillow with a flashlight in one hand, and tears streaming down her face. When I tried to take the flashlight from her she created a terrible resistance, and so I let her keep the light, you see, since it was such comfort to her having it. I never told anyone," said Sister Paulette, a mischievous smile twitching the edges of her lips, "but the very next day I went up to her and gave her a whole box of flashlight batteries, and I told her that when these were used up I would give her some more. It was one of those rare occasions when I was sure I had communicated with her, for as she took the box from me there were tears in her eyes."

Again there was silence for a second, and then the superintendent said gravely, "So, that's it, Sister Paulette. You have just clarified a very great mystery for me. I wondered why it was that you kept requisitioning flashlight batteries week after week!"

The nuns laughed and giggled, rustling in their chairs, their wimples shaking on their heads. Sister Paulette's cheeks puffed out ominously, then became studded with dimples as she blushed like an awkward teen-ager.

I looked around the room, relaxed, and, at the same time exhilarated. These people were real, all right, and I had learned what I was seeking. To the children—hypersensitive to such language of the heart, and often so much more knowing than we think—they would be as real, too. Only more so. I knew I was going to see lots more of pale Sister Paulette, with her shy, hooded eyes.

As the meeting came to an end, I stood up to leave. Instantly, with a quick swishing of material and a sort of sighing of the air shaken by sixty white-winged heads, the sisters rose as one.

In the best manner I could muster at that moment I asked—I think I begged—them to remain seated while I left the room. I was gratified to see that, with smiles on their faces, they proceeded to do just that, as I turned and left. My last sight was of the rows of orderly, untouched scratch pads.

7

Sister Margaret rose to greet me as I went into the Social Services Department a few days later. This department was in a wing of the Institution, employing seven social workers dealing with the children and their families, two experienced supervisors, and . . . Sister Margaret.

As she moved from behind her desk to meet me, I noticed that she was less tall than many of the nuns, a woman in her early thirties, with a round face, and full, mobile mouth. She was good-looking by any standards, yet of an eagerness and hesitant femininity of manner I associate more with the heroines of nineteenth-century Russian novels than with New York City today. She was the social services director and extremely easy to talk to, since she was so diffident and yielding.

She described the kind of work her social workers did, both with the children and with their families, and repeatedly emphasized the shortage of skilled and trained personnel to help. Far too many children—"cases"—had to be assigned to each social worker.

Here she touched in me a responsive chord. In my opinion, mental disorders among children and adolescents were becoming the major human issue of our country, perhaps of our time. I told her of reports I had read estimating that half a million American children suffered from some form of mental illness, a figure that represented only a fraction of those of our young suffering broader emotional disturbances.

"Take the case of Laura," I said. "It's an object lesson, really. So many children show early signs of emotional distress, and nothing will ever be done for them—until it's too late. Sometimes it almost seems to me preferable that a child have some visible physical symptoms, rather than go on suffering silently within itself."

I had talked heatedly about a pet peeve, unsure perhaps how a nun viewed the whole spectrum of mental health. But from the warmth in Sister Margaret's dark and limpid eyes I could see that she needed no convincing.

"You're right, Doctor, there are all too many of them," she said, in her somewhat abashed way of talking. "If a child has a rash or a broken arm or even just a common cold, no one denies it help. But when it has an emotional disturbance the general appearance may be just like any other child, and it's hard to convince people then." She paused briefly, as if uncertain whether to go on. Then she plunged: "It's not always so easy for us here to persuade those above us, as you might think. Some of the older sisters are quite resistant to change." Her lashes moved. "Spare the rod and spoil the child, you know."

"In cases like Laura's," I went on, after I had digested these soft hints, "we're really dealing with psychological crimes committed against children by their parents. We ought to change the language. The reactions of these youngsters to overwhelming experiences is much what a soldier experiences in war."

"Yes, let's call it combat fatigue, shall we?" she said, nodding with alacrity and then grinning generously. "But I must take you through to see Mrs. Clancy now."

Sister Margaret was anxious for me to meet some of her staff and then to talk with one of her supervisors, Mrs. Clancy, who was also Laura's social worker. As I followed the nun's robes out of the office, I knew that I had seldom talked about my personal crusade with such intensity. It was as if this woman had drawn it out of me. I realized that the Institution was only too aware of the role that chance played in the lives of their charges. For Laura luck had come in the form of lack of a state hospital bed. But there were other Lauras still living with their parents, and such would find few resources available for help. Not only were our mental health clinics and residential treatment centers now obliged to be highly selective, restricted to those that "can benefit," but existing facilities focused help on those who sought it, who were basically intelligent, and had intact families. Quite obviously, then, the vast majority of disturbed children from seriously impoverished or broken homes tend to be ineligible for assistance in our present clinical facilities.

"We can do a whole lot more for disturbed children today than most people think," I assured the dark robes swirling beside me down that empty passage. "Like you sisters here. Regardless of race or creed. The trouble is, the community leaves all the responsibility to the professional. It's an incredible social problem, and concerns everyone."

"It certainly does." Then she turned her wide face on mine. "We're so glad you've come to help with Laura, Doctor."

She smiled again, her face lighting as if from within. "Whatever you say is needed for her, please know that we'll do our level best to get it."

I was never to forget those words. At the time I said, "I'm sure you will," but it was mostly to myself, since she had just preceded me into the most chaotic office I have ever seen in my life.

The floor was stacked with cartons of documents, file folders leaked their papers everywhere, cabinets yawned, and one wall was tapestried with dusty books and bound volumes of professional journals. From behind a desk, in parts almost shoulder-high in tottering papers and correspondence, a rawboned, freckle-faced woman stood up with a cup of coffee in one hand and a lighted cigarette in the other.

"Smoking gives you cancer," was her greeting.

"You don't seem to mind." I laughed.

"Around these parts," she retorted briskly, "everyone needs a vice and this happens to be mine. Here." She held out one of three packs of king-sized cigarettes littering the disaster of her desk. It really looked as if a tornado had hit it. "Do you?"

"I do," I said. "Thanks."

"My reserve tank," she replied, lighting up another for herself, though her last was but half smoked down.

Sister Margaret gradually got to present me, in more formal detail, and Mrs. Clancy's cracked lips gave a grin that seemed to embrace the room. Her eyes widened as she said, "So you're the doc who's going to take care of my Laura."

"Guilty," I said.

I knew I was going to get along with Mrs. Clancy. She was one of a hardy, overworked, underpaid breed—social workers. In her late forties, she had already spent over twenty years at the Institution.

While she talked, she moved about with quick steps, knocking over a few cases and chairs and sending folders flying. She was wound like a top, a woman of amazing energy.

There are people who like to work in a general atmosphere of subdued pandemonium, and Mrs. Clancy was one of them. In all my years of dealing with her I never knew her once to lose a single document or record. Most of the time she was way ahead in the tedious documentations required by our cases. And wherever she moved she carried that cup of wine-dark coffee with her, like a banner, slopping from it as she made some point. How often in the years ahead I was to think of that coffee cup and ash-heavy cigarette as the symbols of dedication. The mere smell of coffee in a corridor still reminds me of Mrs. Clancy.

"You need a schedule," she told me, coming out of a side office at me like a train.

"Okay," I said, "if you say so."

So the three of us sat down and worked out a schedule of when I would see Laura regularly.

"Twelve copies," snapped Mrs. Clancy, priming the platen of her antediluvian typewriter as if it were the barrel of a gun. "Here goes for a first draft."

From Sister Margaret's surreptitious smile I could tell this was house routine—in this department, at any rate. Later I was to learn that Mrs. Clancy's schedules were a standing Institution joke. Distributed to the various offices by intra-mural nun-mail, they were rarely consulted thereafter. In actual fact, Mrs. Clancy was a fervid foe of impersonal routine and played everything by a very sensitive ear. But she would insist on her schedules.

So I said good-bye to our "organization woman," puffing at about the eighth cigarette since I had been introduced to her, and followed Sister Margaret to meet the only person in the chain around Laura I had so far not seen. This was the neuropsychiatrist.

Dr. Clemente was about to leave his office for the day when Sister Margaret showed me in. Having done so, the nun excused herself for her duties and left me with him.

Dr. Clemente's office was a model of decorum. In fact, I could see no evidence of paper-work activity about it at all. Barring two telephones, and a packet of Tums, the steel desk seemed virginal.

Dr. Clemente had thick hair, still dark, growing low off his forehead, and he wore a shiny silk suit. I judged him to be about fifty. Sister Margaret had told me that he was employed on a consultant basis and paid out of Institution "funds." He came about twice a week.

We chatted awhile and I found him affable enough, though obviously eager to be off. While I talked his eyes flicked like a lizard's to his watch. Finally, with a smiling shake of his head, he lowered his tone a trifle conspiratorially and said, "Look. Let me tell you. There isn't an awful lot you can do for most of these kids."

"No?"

"No. It's sad but you have to face facts." He turned up his thick palms in an expressive manner.

Perhaps his attitude stung me. I said, "Well, I've decided to give one of the girls some psychotherapy all the same."

"Which one?" he asked, his eyes narrowing.

"Laura," I said.

His face creased in the look of someone who has just seen something unpleasant on his pocket handkerchief. "You serious?"

"Never more so."

He gave a huge shrug and threw out his arms, splaying his palms. "Why waste time . . . ?" He broke off and addressed me earnestly, with all the weight of his years. "Young man, I've been coming to this place a long, long time. Let me tell you, there are kids who could profit from therapy, yes. Sure, I don't deny it. But Laura?"

"I'm treating her now," I said, and since I did not want to get angry, or even into an argument about it, I moved to the door to leave. He shot another glance at his watch.

In fairness, I must say that Dr. Clemente offered to give me any help I might need. But he all too obviously shared the philosophy I was opposing—rescue those who show most likelihood of profiting by it. To date Laura had shown no signs of even minimal adjustment.

"It's your choice," he said, with another smiling shrug as he shook my hand.

Hurrying off, I glanced at my watch. That evening I had appointments to keep in my own practice, but I wanted first to check that everything was ready for Laura's next visit to me in the new office I had been assigned.

This, too, faced into a long, high passage but was smaller, more cheerfully decorated; neatly distributed on shelves and tables were all the materials I had requested from the superintendent. The gray granite walls seemed far away in this almost cozy place. Then came a jangling clang. Nuns started swinging into the corridor, their robes billowing about them as they made smartly for the far end.

As more of them poured out, clicking their rosaries and moving at a brisk clip, I assumed this was a fire drill. And if I remembered one thing from high school, it was that you don't talk in fire drill. I guessed I had to participate. So I followed the general surge, finally descending a set of steps wedged in a phalanx of sisters, each silent, head lowered. Suddenly we all made a sharp turn through double doors and I found myself in the brightly candlelit institutional chapel.

The nuns filed to their places on either side of the nave and it dawned on me now that the bell had been for one of their religious offices—vespers, or was it compline? Once more, all sixty seemed to be there. The great doors closed behind me, and I was left standing to one side. A priest came in, with two acolytes, and a service was soon under way.

After some minutes of this the priest, a white-haired oldster wearing pince-nez, came resolutely toward me. I confess my heart started to pound. Bending forward stiffly in his white surplice, he declared, "Now would you lead us in the Second Mystery?"

"What did you say, Father?"

But it was no good. He repeated his invitation (if you could call it such) and by this time more and more nuns were staring at me. In desperation I raised one hand and gestured to the side of my neck. In a hoarse whisper that I hoped didn't sound too stagey, I got out, "I do have this terrible throat today."

I thought he looked at me in some disgust before he turned and retraced his stately steps. At the end of the service I moved quickly toward the big doors out.

"Let me help you," said a whisper at my side, and a nun expertly sprang the latch. I passed out with her, perspiring.

Language

"I'm so sorry you have a sore throat, Doctor, I do hope it will clear up soon. Perhaps it was a slight case of . . . combat fatigue." I peeked under the headdress. Sister Margaret was walking beside me.

8

A few days later I sat in my new room waiting for Laura. Already the place had taken on a friendliness I would have believed impossible or, at best, most unlikely that first day. The nun who met me at the door seemed particularly receptive now, and everyone I passed on the way to my office was friendly, smiling, and courteous. I realized they were becoming more comfortable with me, as I was with them.

Pale, austere Sister Paulette, impulsive Sister Margaret, chain-smoking Mrs. Clancy—so many warm hearts pulsed within these gray walls that when I arrived now I began to see that forbidding barbed wire as *keeping the others out!* Yes, the intense affection of these nuns needed protection, it was plain, from our predatory world outside, one that honored the acquisition of money rather than self-sacrifice and was content to ignore this hidden example of personal devotion, lost in a city of over eight million. But it would never have occurred to the nuns to ask for notice.

While I waited for Laura to come to meet me in my new office, I reviewed the story of her life over and over. For a while all I could see was a child being held in a nun's arms night after night. Why should Laura trust me? Why give up the security of her isolation for the dangers of a new relationship fraught with all kinds of unknowns? What could I offer? What say? Above all, how could I respond to her silence—and finally tempt her out of it? As I waited I began to be possessed by increasing self-doubt. Perhaps I had taken on more than I knew. For reassurance I searched back into my own life and experience.

An inner struggle with isolation in my own childhood had taught me that loneliness seeks not its own cure. Far from it. It is more like a vicious cycle, for the fear of being hurt is often stronger than the need for reassurance, with the result that the lonely child does not dare to risk the ridicule of others. In Laura's case I had to multiply this a thousand-fold. Furthermore, my experience as a psychoanalyst had been concentrated on working with deprived and neglected patients. So, all in all, putting together my own education and my analysis, I felt the time had come to use everything I'd got in an attempt to reach this child.

Unlike other professions, perhaps, psychoanalysis is a waiting game. A psychoanalyst may have to bide his time for years for any indication of success. In fact, we sometimes have no way of knowing whether our patients' lives turn out significantly better as a result of our work with them. An engineer, doctor, or teacher can usually see some immediate fruits of his labor. With Laura I knew it was going to be a long battle, but I was ready to invest my time and energy without expectations of any sort. By now I had convinced myself that, after what she'd been through, anything Laura gave of herself would be a gift indeed. I leaned forward in my chair and stared down the hallway, empty at that moment. The minutes ticked by.

I glanced at my watch. The nuns had already shown themselves to me as a hyperpunctual group and, sure enough, within seconds of Mrs. Clancy's schedule, Laura made her appearance at the end of the long bare corridor, with the same sister supporting her.

Once again she walked with her head bowed, leaning heavily on the wall, her left hand to her face. With her disheveled hair, crouched posture, and general lack of vitality, it might have been a very old woman coming toward me rather than a child who should have been enjoying the full delights of youthful life. The sister brought her into my office, nodded to me, and left us alone.

Laura sat lifeless, bunched in the chair. Again her nose was heedlessly running. So motionless did she sit that I felt I could almost hear her heart beating. Sound already muffled by the snow outside, the silence in the room now seemed amplified, enormous. And then I saw that she was crying.

Great tears welled up in her eyes and lolled down her scarred cheeks. They seemed to speak more loudly than any tongue to me at that moment, mute evidence of who-knew-what inner agony—but at least a communication. I watched them slip down her skin, and fall on her lap.

"Hello, Laura," I said. "Remember me?"

She made no move, but I told myself that the tears symbolized a soul within that frozen shell of immobility. Her despair was an act of life. An active negativity was affirming itself in front of me.

"Have a good Christmas, Laura?" I asked.

Such was the beginning of hundreds of sessions between us. They went on week after week, month after month, year after year. And at the start the pattern of the first was the pattern of them all. I was talking to a blank brick wall.

Each time I saw her I greeted her with as much genuine warmth as I felt I had for her. Sincerity was all-important if she was to trust me. But there was no change in her behavior, her mood, or her mannerisms. Occasionally she would wipe her nose, and as often she would not. Only the tears told me there was a life inside, someone I had to reach.

I decided on a structure of three ways in which to spend time with my patient. First, I would talk to her about all of the things that were happening outside the walls of the Institution. I would move around the room, look out the window, describe what I saw outside. Second, I would expose her gradually to the materials in the room, the toys and games. Third, there would be times when I would be silent myself, and sit, and wait. And then it was my own heart I heard beating.

It was nothing very technical. I spoke to Laura as anyone speaks to a child. I chose simple words, made my descriptions as vivid as possible, full of images.

"Gee, there's a fire engine stopped across the street. That's really red. Isn't it, though. F.D.N.Y. Anyone'd think it'd just been painted yesterday. . . ."

I was not new to play therapy, and there was nothing particularly new about my approach to Laura, with the possible exception that, of all the hundreds of hours of play therapy I had clocked up with disturbed children, she gave me the least to go on.

A typical play-therapy room might contain such materials as a doll house and a doll family, doll furniture, toy soldiers and animals, playhouse chairs, a table, doll bed, and cooking utensils and the like. Rag dolls are also good, puppets, a puppet screen, crayons, clay, finger paints, sand, toy telephones, almost anything that will lend itself to *expressive play*, the furniture of a kindergarten with emphasis on materials as vehicles through which the child can express emotion. If only Laura had been tempted to use some of the soft, colorful paint I set before her I might have had some access to her inner emotions. Since her motor behavior was virtually nil I was again denied further potential clues as to infantilism and the like. When working with a child like this, an analyst notes all forms of orientation to the external situation, and indeed all purposeful movements.

I have had since those days the case of one disturbed boy, aged seven, who for many sessions of an hour would simply dangle a rope from one hand and occasionally twirl it without apparent meaning. He once noticed a statue of a horse on a mantel of my office and asked to play with it. The horse had a small chain around its neck and the boy's fascination was with this rather than with the horse. He sat on the floor and twirled the chain, repeating this ritualistic behavior when I returned the rope to him. There were other rites, too, such as a tensed bringing of his hands together and blowing on them in front of his face, cyclical rituals that became more pronounced when I attempted to administer a Rorschach, and after which there would be an improvement in rapport.

So, in dealing with deeply disturbed children, the analyst has to work on very small hints. He must take his cue from the patient. But even these small hints were denied me with Laura in those long, long hours. The administration of a Rorschach test was out of the question. She wouldn't so much as have looked at the cards, let alone make any verbal response.

In short, I had to make up a dialogue out of a monologue, something that might involve her in some way. Usually almost any child invited into a playroom will investigate curiously. Even without words there will nearly always be some activity that will, when repeated, spell out something. Or there might be, as is the case with one of my young patients at the present time, an obsession about the cleanliness of the objects being handled. Walking in itself—the placing of a child's steps—can give clues to those schooled in such therapy. Laura walked only with assistance.

Each time she entered my office I watched her eyes. They might linger over an empty glass that had not been there on her previous visit, or some cookies sent up to me from the Institution kitchen. I might notice the tiniest change of a reaction in a new way I lit a cigarette—or pretended that I couldn't find my matches, when they were staring me in the face the whole time. Again, I would drop the box near her, hoping that perhaps she might bend and pick it up. But without speech I was especially handicapped, for it is here, by making up a dialogue for doll people, say, that a child can express his emotions and problems. I chose toys and dolls as symbols of Laura's life and sometimes provided for her a little apron or smock so that she might feel freer to use the paints without being restricted by the fear of soiling her clothes. There was fortunately a washbasin at hand, and I noted that the windows had protective wire screens on them. But it was hard to make any headway at all.

Sometimes I would try to use street sounds to catch her interest. The clanking of garbage cans or a siren. "That means the fire engine's going off now, Laura," I would say. "It's done its job and that's to clear the traffic out of the way so that it can get back quickly."

And so on, and so on. Not only did I ransack my brain, and my ever-diminishing vocabulary, to picture the street for her, but I tried to introduce more general abstractions, like winter, showing how it froze the snow to the limbs of trees, like the tinsel decorations she had seen in the corridors that Christmas.

Smoke funneled out of a chimney, and I'd tell her how this meant that all the people inside were being protected from the cold by the furnace burning oil. I pictured for her a file of children, bundled like polar bears, being led across the street by a very unsteady nun, clutching an umbrella, her headdress built up into a minor snowdrift of its own.

As winter gave way to spring, and there was no change in the child before me, I thought of her own analogy to the new season, and tried to take courage from it, for was not she, too, waiting to be born, and come to life?

After all, for twelve years now she hadn't really lived. I tried to use her name more and more, struggling to make what I had to say seem interesting, involving, and as I went along I interjected more and more questions in the hope that one day, somehow or another, she would get caught up in answering, if only to herself. And each day I saw her led out silently by the sister I thought of the words of that poet who understood children so well, William Wordsworth:

. . . the marble index of a mind
Forever voyaging through strange seas of thought alone.

The normal curiosity of a child Laura's age would be to explore such a room filled with toys and games. Obviously, Laura was still incapable of normal curiosity. So each session I would bring some of the materials to the desk and place them, quite casually, directly in her line of vision.

Once the merry-go-round seemed to produce a startled response in her eyes, as the carrousel music poured out of the box and the tiny horses moved up and down with the revolutions of the platform. As a result, I played the musical carrousel for her at some point in every session. Those few chords echoed through my dreams, and through my nightmares, too! But the music was an important third sound for both of us, a relief from my having to verbalize. Words are the mind's attempt to order itself, and Laura was not yet willing to risk this lost ability on uncharted and "strange seas of thought alone."

All in all, I was glad to see the end to that long, cold winter. The days lengthened and there was a stirring of life within the community. Children came and went in the street, hopping and skipping. Men could be seen polishing their cars, women in bright dresses shopping in a more leisurely way, and as the weather became warmer the first old people sauntered out to the benches under the still-bare trees and read their papers. I decided to take my patient for a stroll outside. Frankly, by this time, I was running out of things to say to Laura.

Protected in the center of the Institution were some pleasant grounds: playgrounds with swings, children's areas, slides and seesaws, the usual thing. It was also a place where in summer the nuns came to walk for a few minutes of an evening when they could find time. There were some well-grown plane trees and plots of tended flowers. It was a place more in keeping with a child's world, I thought, than the inside of an office; and if Laura wasn't going to talk with me she might as well, I reasoned, be silent outside, in the year's first sun.

I walked with her very slowly. I was glad to notice that she managed to get along without support from a wall or from the arm that at first I offered her. I was encouraged by this slight degree of freedom. I talked to her all the time, pointing out this tree or that early flower. And as we walked the other children would run up and speak to me. They all seemed bursting with energy and eager to talk. I watched Laura when they did this, but she made no response.

On the whole, while the other children tried to be friendly to my little patient, they couldn't help noticing her infirmities. They would ask her to come jump rope, or play ball, or join in their hopscotch game. They could not know that these activities, so full of fun for them, were terrors to Laura. They were part of the real world, and of that social interchange, and competition, that her young spirit had shied away from. However much she might have wanted to join in, she was doomed to remain the observer, too frightened to risk the chance of losing, for what would be lost for her would be no game at all, but a sanctuary against being hurt.

Indeed, it was not always that Laura could have surrendered her shell with impunity. There was the day when I went to meet her in the grounds only to find a group of girls teasing her, mocking and making faces, fingers stuck out from the sides of their ears. "Hunchback . . . hunchback," I heard. "Hunchback of Notre Dame!" I quickly dispersed them.

Only two incidents gave me cheer during those first months outside. I discovered that Laura seemed somewhat attracted to the swings and so I would push her gently as she grasped the long chains at the sides of the seat. Unlike other children, she made no effort to swing herself, with movement of body or legs. I hoped she might, but she just sat. And I pushed.

The second event was slightly more cheering. I discovered that Laura had one thing in common with all children and that was a love of candy. So every day I arrived at the Institution to see her I loaded up with candy bars—Mars, Hershey's, Crunchee, Chunky, Bit-o-Honey—I got to know the whole gamut of what helps keep dentists in business.

"Tchee, you certainly go for candy, Doc," murmured the owner of the little stationery store I now stopped at before taking the subway ride or drive out.

These candy bars had a way of involving Laura in our first real communication. I would offer her one, and she would accept it. It was, when all was said and done, the only thing she had accepted from me so far. And then she would have to carry on the communication in the movements of unwrapping the candy, screwing up the paper, and tossing it aside, before finally placing the oversweet goo in her mouth.

I'm afraid calorie counting had to go by the board. It was, of course, about the most elementary form of relationship possible. But, sensitized to such by hours of silence, I felt we had broken some barrier, and that this tolerant acceptance of my gift, together with that speechless flow of tears, indicated that somewhere within Laura was a living person.

9

The sun was hot that year. It beat on my back each afternoon I made for the Institution now, shining on the fronts of fruit stalls and funeral parlors and sawdust-strewn butcher shops in that neighborhood I had got to know so well. And there were days when it seemed to pour with especial weight on the giant ad in the corner pharmacist's, a peerlessly girdled girl laughing to screaming pitch under the general rubric Turn Their Heads.

As I loaded up with candy at the stationery store the owner shifted the wet stub of cigar in his mouth, scratched at a white-shirted armpit, said, "Think y'can keep this up, Doc?"

"What?"

I was always self-conscious about buying the junk, and I'm sure my sentiments showed. The man merely pointed at my handful of garish horrors.

"You know best, Doc. Y'can only live once, I guess."

You can only live once.

I made for the iron fretwork of the subway opening. As I descended, stuffing the loot for Laura in my pockets, hoping the candy bars wouldn't melt too much, I reflected that usually I rejoiced at summer activity in the city, visible in the bakeries and fruit stores, the cigar stands and shoeshine bars that seemed to come alive then. Drapes flapped out of windows like sails, girls sat on fire escapes and sills, and the wings of pigeons on the sidewalk seemed to beat strongly, as if with a vigor acquired by the season. Perhaps all I need add is that I am a confirmed tennis buff.

This summer, however, was going to be different. For it was to bring an interruption in my sessions with Laura. Each mid-June the Institution moved its personnel and children to the seashore, in an effort to provide for these lonely kids the sense of going to a summer camp. Each previous summer Laura had been to camp, and this was clearly far from the moment to break the routine. A small core of three or four nuns were left to look after the Institution.

Not wanting to get my candies crushed, I stood rather than sat in the subway car and listened to the talk around me. A heavy man with blond hair, carrying his jacket on his arm and mopping his brow as if it were a floor, was saying, "Senn'ty, senn'ty-six . . . I'm telling you, you have to take a few points and then get out. . . ."

"Like I was saying," rejoined his neighbor, whose face I could not see, "fifteen, twenty thousand, the whole secret of the market is *timing*."

"There are guys who can triple their . . ."

When I emerged, the sky over Staten Island and the Bay was gray, almost greenish where the incoming sea bisected it. Thundershowers had been announced before nightfall, and I was glad. It would clear the air. That evening I was scheduled to give a talk in another part of the city and, since it was about problems of retarded children, I thought some of the nuns might like to come. I had extended an open invitation through the superintendent.

As I walked toward the Institution I thought of how it had changed for me since that snowy day Dorothy had first brought me to it. Now it looked almost friendly, so associated with human kindness had it become in my mind. A group of kids in T-shirts was fooling round a hydrant, which a cop had just turned on for them. A big, tan boy had fitted an old beer can, perforated with holes, over the jet and the children were capering like monkeys in the writhing streams of artificial rain. A barefoot girl was calling, "*Mira! Mira!*" I would even miss the neighborhood this summer.

I met Laura in the grounds, walked her a little in the steamy heat. We watched children scampering through colored tunnels and playing in the sandpit under the supervision of a nun whose robes must have been giving her a built-in sauna, but who remained patiently cheerful all the time. I swung Laura awhile.

"I brought you some candy," I said at last. "It's kind of soft by now, I guess."

It was. Nonetheless, Laura's fingers accepted the offering, took off the paper wrapping, and conveyed it to her mouth. Had I for a split second been able to detect a smile there? It was the year's reward I gave myself, at any rate, as her jaws slowly, but quite definitely, masticated, their rhythm increasing, I considered, with relish—the symbol becoming the thing symbolized. My blood was pulsing. Yes, I was sure I was getting through to her. I took the sticky paper from her right hand and rolled it up and threw it in a litter bin.

"I won't see you till September, Laura," I said.

Silence.

"But I will see you then."

We strolled under the almost cold shade of a tree.

"I do want you to know that. You'll be going to camp . . . and you'll have a great time there, I'll bet. It's by the sea. You remember, Laura? You like it, don't you? And when you come back in September, I'll see you again. Okay?"

The nun who had brought her to me was waiting on the stone seat, telling her beads. Sometimes I felt these tirelessly busy sisters simply used their rosaries functionally, as a method of keeping their fingers employed, perhaps a little like those Greek *kombolai*, or worry beads, used by Athenian businessmen and dockers alike. She took Laura under her wing with a smile. I stood and watched them go. Was there just a little, perhaps a fraction, more self-support in Laura's gait?

"Good-bye, Laura," I said.

I did not have to add, "Take care." Someone would do that, all right.

I turned and made quickly for my office, where I had previously set up meetings with sisters Paulette and Margaret, both of whom were going to the camp on Long Island and to whom I wished to say good-bye for the summer. I had personally invited both to the talk I was giving that evening at six.

As I sat and waited for a farewell visit from Laura's group mother I wondered if I was being, in a manner of speaking, "conned" by the unshakable faith of these women into seeing improvements in my patient that simply weren't there.

Sister arrived punctually at three o'clock, not a split second earlier or later, but calmly and softly as the Institution clock chimed the hour. By now I knew you could set your watch at the movements of the nuns, yet this degree of timing struck me as slightly superhuman. I rose and offered her the chair next to my desk. Then I went and closed the door behind her.

Sister Paulette looked pale and a trifle drawn, I thought, in need of rest. Her eyes seemed very deeply set, watching me as I moved. All I knew about this reticent woman was that she had a strong love for Laura. It was important for me to get to know her better, learn something of the atmosphere she created in her division. For just as a mother makes a certain climate in her home, so, of course, a nun in charge of children plays a significant part in their emotional environment, one that reflects the character of the person in charge. That afternoon I was to learn something about the climate Sister Paulette provided, but I did not bargain on a basic lesson in religious etiquette as well.

As I sat down, Sister Paulette stood up. With a graceful, semi-apologetic glide she went back to the door and opened it halfway.

There was no air-conditioning in the Institution and my room seemed unbearably stuffy. It must have been doubly worse for a nun in full attire. However, it was a professional habit of mine to ensure privacy at such discussions. So I got up again and opened the window, murmuring, "If I'm going to smoke in here, Sister, I think you'll be happier this way." And as inconspicuously as possible I closed the door behind her back, before resuming my seat at the desk.

When I had done so, however, I glanced up—only to find Sister Paulette opening it halfway again. She resumed her seat and with the closest I ever heard her come to a giggle, said, "You see, Doctor, it's a rule that we must leave the door open whenever we enter a place where there is a man. I hope I don't annoy you, but we do have these rules we have to obey."

I smiled and assured her it was quite all right, but that I myself was guided by an inner leaning to the contrary.

"Actually," I said, "rules like that aren't part of my frame of reference at all, Sister. Do you think they really help?"

She bent forward, the light frown pleating her forehead again. "I beg your pardon?"

"Surely they tend to make for a feeling of mistrust among you, rather than otherwise?"

"Mistrust?"

She looked genuinely puzzled, even worried, that she could not sensibly answer my question; so I at once went on to another point.

Sister Paulette was of the kingdom of heaven. She was a reticent person who lived her humble existence without questions and without doubt. Her obedience was to God. We started earnestly discussing Laura. The nun opened out at once.

To start with, what I had anticipated seemed all too true. Laura was pretty much the same as she always had been. I was simply kidding myself if I felt otherwise. The mocking smile of Dr. Clemente seemed to hover over us as we chatted.

Second, I again ran up against this conviction on the sister's part that Laura was alive inside, and just could not break through to the world. Secretly I had this impression myself, and for this reason I prodded the nun about it. I wanted to hear her articulate something comforting, something I could hang onto in the months ahead; but it was all too plain that for Sister Paulette the matter was one of pure intuition, at one with her faith in God.

"I don't know how it is, Doctor," she said, struggling to help me understand, "it's just that when there are certain days that Laura is very sad, I always know it."

"By the expression on her face?"

"Not that only. Oh, it's so difficult to express. We've been together so many years by now. The fact that she can't speak is only truly a barrier for those who don't know her. For me," she concluded proudly, "it does not matter. I know what is in her heart."

I dropped my eyes. As the nun went on, I thought how illogical this information really was. Technically it was no help at all. But yet I believed her, it made sense, in the context in which we were. As she talked on, her strictly chiseled face fixed on mine, I understood her immense love for this lost girl. It was the total devotion of any mother for her handicapped infant.

The nun's patience was immeasurable, a tribute to that obedience to the rules I had criticized in her. She had never pushed Laura into any unwanted activity, never rebuked her—as understandably she might have—for any failure to involve herself with the others. The child and nun were one, I realized—outsiders, oddballs, misfits if you will. In spite of all the many children in the Institution who demanded care, in spite of the limited number of staff available, this woman had somehow or other contrived to find time to give so much of herself to a wanting, suffering girl. Her intuition had taken her through the barriers, and drawn curtains of silence, into a manifest communion of spirit. Suddenly I glanced up and received perhaps the most profound shock of that year. Sister Paulette was weeping.

The nun had read my thoughts. Her lined face was pushed forward, jaw set. She looked almost old. Large tears lolled down her cheeks.

"I assure you . . . I *promise* you, Doctor, one day Laura will be better. Don't give up on her. Please. I am as sure as sure can be—one day Laura will talk and play like other children."

"But we both agree, there's been no improvement in her behavior."

"It'll take a long time, Doctor, for, you see, she was hurt at such a tender age."

I smiled. "I won't give up, Sister," I said.

She dried her eyes hurriedly and I seized my chance. This was the moment to broach something that had been in my mind for several months already. I leaned forward and put it as diffidently, yet as sincerely, as I knew how.

"She's going to need medical assistance," I said. "I'm convinced that Laura's appearance is a vital factor in her mental health."

"An operation?" she asked dubiously.

I nodded; and to my surprise she came back at once, "You're right."

Encouraged by how the nun had sensed it, too, I went on. "Her eyes, for one thing."

"And then her back, also, Doctor."

I paused. "The trouble is . . ."

"What?"

"It'll be very expensive."

"We'll manage, somehow."

"How?"

The nun hooded her eyes again. "When the time comes," was all she would say.

I looked at Sister Paulette keenly. I was convinced she had no idea of how she would get money for Laura's physical improvement, but get it somehow she would. It is a tragedy that if any institutionalized child needs specialized medical care for physical survival, there is no question of getting it; but if such care is important principally to mental well-being, it will not be considered vital. Such cases are considered cosmetic. I was almost sure there'd be no chance of getting Laura's vision defect classified as an essential of her health. I spoke in some exasperation.

"It'll mean the services of specialists, Sister."

"Ah, no doubt."

"Have you any faintest idea," I pressed, "of how much major operative care costs in a big city hospital today?"

"I'll get up a collection, Doctor."

"Who from?"

"Amongst my friends."

I stared at her speechlessly for a second.

"Or we'll borrow from a bank, you see, and pay back over a period of time. You can do that, you know," she told me consolingly, sensing my mood. Outside a bell rang and she stood up hurriedly. As she did so she patted my hand. "Don't worry, Doctor, we'll find a way. When the time comes. Just you wait." Then she leaned across the desk. "Every day I pray for Laura to get well, and my prayers have brought you here to help her, Doctor. So I shall just have to pray a little bit harder for the money we're going to need, shan't I? . . . Have a good summer now."

And with a swirl of her robes she swept out.

10

I glanced at my watch and started putting my records away safely for the summer break. My schedule was a tight one if I was to make the meeting that evening in a collected manner.

Sister Margaret was late. As I have remarked, life in the Institution went pretty much by the book, with all appointments and functions on the dot. Frankly, if this had not been the case, with the demands of a hundred and fifty girls to be met daily, chaos would have come again. For most of the nuns life was a constant rush and Sister Margaret and I had spoken only very briefly since that first meeting many months before.

Behind her friendly smile and warm greeting was a routine of life in which she and her staff were constantly racing against time to accomplish an endless rote of assignments that "absolutely cannot wait." It was little short of incredible how each nun smoothed out the wrinkle of every problem involving the diversified needs of all the children thrust together under this roof. And as soon as one day's problems were solved, the next morning brought a new set. As Mrs. Clancy put it to me once, "Each night I leave I check: Do I have my shoes on? Have I had anything to eat? Do I know where I'm going?"

I'm sure Mrs. Clancy knew the answer to all three questions every night, but her point was good. Sister Margaret was an unusual half hour late, explaining when she arrived that she had been in the middle of reading a story to a four-year-old, laid up in the infirmary, and both the child and she had had to see how the story ended. The only other time I knew Sister Margaret to be late for a meeting was an occasion that elicited the following explanation: "You see, Doctor, I was with some of the very young ones and one of them pulled off my headdress, and then it took a little time getting the oatmeal out of my hair." She looked at me softly. "Try not to be discouraged, Doctor," was what she said. I think I stared at her blankly.

On this occasion I did most of the listening as the soft-spoken sister told me her tales of how very few nuns there were trained in the field of social work and psychology, especially in view of the complex problems created by the children in the Institution. This was the first outspoken comment on the shortcomings of the nuns, freely and frankly admitted, and by one of their own number, that I had yet encountered. Here was a trained psychiatric social worker, with exceptional experience in working with disturbed children, letting down her hair to me—if I may be pardoned the expression of a nun. I found myself face to face with an extraordinary insight into individual motivations, and the causes of disturbed behavior, all taken by this demurely decorous and very handsome woman as a matter of course.

It was, in a sense, the opposite in attitude to that of Sister Paulette. The director of the Social Work Department was by no means certain she was going to heaven. Sister Margaret was very much a woman. Her intensity derived from this world, rather than from the next. For her the wearing of the habit did not turn everyone into a miracle worker, or convert their flaws into virtues.

She was a genuine maverick, an independent thinker within her strict order, yet fully eventuated and unafraid of her opinion as a person. In the medieval period she would, perhaps, have been typical of the attitude of anticlaustration, of the active over the contemplative life, of which Sister Paulette was such a shining example. She might even have been a Chaucerian Wife of Bath or, at any rate, closer to her in spirit than to the Nun of Chaucer's tales. It must be rare to find a person who can combine the sophistication and intelligence of a woman living in the modern world with the rigors of a role strongly rooted in centuries-old tradition.

Sister Margaret never seemed to find these orientations contradictory; she lived on her belief that her religious dedication was reaching out to help other people. She accepted the conventual rules as constructive and personally helpful, and I think that if she had not found them so, she would not have remained. There was no blind obedience in this nun who seemed subtly to move between two worlds with the grace of a swan, reflecting the best of each as she disarmed a rebellious adolescent, comforted a hurt child, or quieted an angry staff member. She remained a marginal individual, with the sensitivity of an artist, the manipulative skill of some feminine Machiavelli, and the humility, yes, of a saint.

As she talked to me about her plans and problems, I could not keep from reflecting how extraordinarily—and ignorantly—lucky the city was to have this tame task force working for it. They were true missionaries and, as such, could have been withdrawn at a moment's notice by the mother general. After we had finished talking about Laura, we chatted about mutual friends—of Dorothy still working hard in the Institutional Field Office, of Dr. Clemente, and others. Our meeting was coming to a close and I realized I would be sad to see the last of Sister Margaret for a while.

"I'm sorry I won't be able to come to your talk tonight, Doctor," she said, "but I simply can't get away."

"That's all right," I said. "Another time."

"Yes, I hope you'll remember to invite me again. It's so good to think you will be back here in the fall, to see Laura some more. But you look as if you need a rest. You have a good vacation, Doctor."

"You too," I echoed automatically. And then I realized that these nuns never took a break themselves. With the others Sister Margaret would be going to help run the camp for the children all summer. Ten days a year the nuns went on retreat, in the contemplation of God, under the auspices of a priest, and this interval of reflection, and spiritual renewal for their battles ahead, was the closest they ever came to any holiday.

Sister Margaret smiled as she read my mind. Half apologetically she said, "It seems the problems of children never take a vacation, doesn't it, Doctor?" She stood up. "I hope your talk goes well. Some of us, I am sure, will be there," she added, as if comforting me.

Twelve were. And I shall never forget it. The talk was sponsored by a professional organization and given in a Manhattan hotel. A dinner was to follow the speeches. As the first speaker started and I saw the twelve nuns in a row, each with a sharpened pencil and white scratch pad, I gave myself a pat on the back for having been instrumental in getting them out of the Institution and interested in other helpful techniques. Neither Sister Margaret nor Sister Paulette was present. The only nun I knew at all was a short, energetic woman called Sister Philomene, who had the reputation of being a crackerjack biology teacher.

The talks were short and without incident—except that one learned speaker, unused to addressing a mike, poured much of his coruscating oratory into a lamp—and the meeting broke up around eight. The audience made their way out, except that is for the twelve sisters, who went on sitting resolutely in their row in the ballroom. When I went back some minutes later to tell them the meeting was adjourned, and they could go, the short nun looked up at me shyly. "You see, Doctor, we aren't allowed to eat in a public place. We couldn't go into the restaurant."

"And it'll be a little late for supper when we do get back," put in another.

I realized they were hungry. It was a tough situation, and I solved it only after some difficulty and a conference with the reception clerk, the general manager, plus, finally, the chef himself. What do you do with twelve hungry nuns who can't go to a restaurant? Well, we found them a small banquet room where they could be by themselves, and a waitress to serve their meal. I forgot about them and joined some colleagues in the main dining room.

It was getting on toward ten o'clock when I said good-bye to these acquaintances. I could hear that the promised thundershower had broken and rain was teeming down. Across the lobby the manager was smiling at me like some Cheshire cat, and with good reason too. He handed me a bill for exactly $113.

"The sisters' dinner," he explained gravely.

I think I must just have stared at it stupidly and said something like, "What on earth did they eat?" But I knew my hand was reaching for my checkbook as his explanations started.

"Fifty dollars for the room, sir. The repast was forty-eight. Fifteen for the special waitress . . . I felt sure you would wish to take care of it yourself, Doctor. Your car registration will be perfectly satisfactory. . . ."

I walked rather sickly out through the revolving doors, and bumped straight into the twelve nuns. They were standing just out of the lashing rain. There was a smell of wet in the air, a tang of still hot, drenched sidewalks.

"We had a delightful dinner," said Sister Philomene. "Thank you so much, Doctor." And she stared eloquently into the rain. They all did.

My breathing coming faster, I began to count. At most I could get three in my car, which left nine to transport back to the Institution. I should have thought of this before.

Back inside the lobby again I was trying to stop the manager from calling a fleet of cabs until I knew exactly, and very precisely, what it was all going to cost (I felt we two were getting to know each other well), when Sister Philomene tapped my shoulder.

"Please don't worry about getting us home, Doctor. We've found a way."

Outside, a long airport limousine had drawn up. It looked as if it could hold a dozen nuns and, by the time I regained the soaking sidewalk, it already held some four or five. I helped them in most cheerfully, closing the door securely on Sister Philomene, who stepped in last. At which point a voice by my side said, "Who's going to pay for this, doc?" The driver stood scratching his head in the rain. "I pull up here. They just start climbing in on me, see."

"They must have thought it was a bus," I tried.

"Yeah. Well, it ain't. This job costs money."

"You can't leave a lot of nuns on the sidewalk in the rain."

"No?" He seemed unconvinced.

I clutched at my straw. "Listen. You a Catholic?"

"Sure."

"Then you can't throw them out. I mean, a bunch of nuns . . ."

The man looked from me to the nuns and from the nuns back to me. Finally he said, "I'll do it for twenty bucks." As I was reaching for my billfold, I was feeling quite happy to think I shouldn't be around *nuns* for a while.

11

That summer I thought about Laura a great deal. By the time I took my first subway ride back to the Institution, I knew I could not give up this case despite the inroads it was making on my own time and practice.

I surfaced on the familiar area blocked by stone, and blemished by lack of color and connection. There was no sense here of what the French call "quarter," as there had been in the neighborhood of Jack Di Salvio and his friends. The projects rose in squadlike clusters, there was a paralysis of vitality in their very enormity, a mute absence of warmth and individuality that, for me now, only underscored the personal poverty and dedication of the nuns.

The smell of coffee greeted me on the way to my office. Mrs. Clancy, Laura's social worker, rounded a bend in the main corridor a moment later, cup in one hand, cigarette in the other.

"Cancer kills," she said, spraying ashes. "How are you, Doctor? Have a good summer?"

"Fine, thanks, Mrs. Clancy. And you?"

It didn't need asking. Here was someone who had actually had a vacation. The big-boned woman was tanned, alert, and energetic. In a month she would look different, obsessed with the problems of her children and how to do best for them. As we strolled down the passage with an easier step than usual here, she told me that nothing had changed with Laura.

At camp she had been the same as ever—apathetic, uncommunicative . . . silent. The children had all come back a few days before and Laura would be brought down to see me at the usual hour. I was slipping back into a routine of which, at that moment, I saw no end.

When I went into my office I found that the place had been given a whole-hearted cleaning, one characteristic of the Institution's thoroughness.

On my desk was a note from the superintendent, formally but cheerfully welcoming me back. And when I opened the folder containing my mail I found a card. It had on it the picture of a prisoner behind bars, a number on his chest, with a caption underneath: "How does it feel to know that you're—WANTED?" I hardly had to look at the signature to know that it came from Sister Margaret.

For the next few minutes I checked the toys and paints, the papers and crayons I would be using in my work with Laura, and had asked for in advance. Everything seemed in order. It was as I sat down that I realized I would need rags.

Having employed this sort of therapy before, I knew all too well that if a child is going to play with finger paint it's just as well to have some rags on hand, unless you want to have your office painted, and sometimes yourself as well. With very small ones you must be careful they don't eat the pink.

When I'd left, there had been a bunch of cleaning rags I'd stored in a little bag in the closet, but like everything else in my room this had been cleaned out of sight. I picked up the phone. The girl at the switchboard, a pleasant brunette putting herself through graduate school nights at N.Y.U., answered.

"Elaine, I wonder if you could have some rags sent to me?" I asked.

The girl's voice paused. "Rags, Doctor?"

"Right."

"I'll see to it at once," came back her rather frigid reply. I thanked her and hung up.

Four minutes later I heard a trundling in the hall. A toothless woman in a faded blue robe peered around my door. "Shall we clean you now, sir?"

Behind her was apparent an obese maintenance man, wearing denims and a disgruntled look, and behind him a mobile cleaning unit containing enough mops, swabs, brooms, rags, pails, wringers, and other equipment to shine up a small skyscraper.

"We're the cleaning unit," said the man. "We'll get it clean in no time."

In a moment the two were dusting my shelves, swabbing down the vinyl floor, and generally filling my office with their impedimenta. I couldn't understand why they chose to clean the room at this particular hour. However, spying a clump of rags on the bottom shelf of the cart, I asked the elderly cleaning woman if I might take them.

"Good God, Doctor," she said, turning to me and audibly gasping, "you don't have to clean your own office. Not here. That's our job."

I explained that such was far from my intention, I simply needed the rags for a child using finger paints, water, and clay.

The man dropped his swab with a clang. "You mean to tell us, you need those rags for the kids?"

"That's right. If you wouldn't mind."

"So it wasn't you as complained to the switchboard operator on us?"

"What do you mean?" I asked.

The woman broke in, "That your room was all horrible filthy and you needed some rags for to clean it."

"Great Scott!" I exclaimed.

I explained the error, and the resultant confusion. It had been generally put about—for I had long ago discovered that the Institution was a beehive—that I was dissatisfied with the cleanliness of my office, and planning to clean it myself.

The maintenance staff had been told to drop everything and do a rush job of the place at once. And when the superintendent sent out an order like that, it tended to be answered promptly.

"I'm terribly sorry," I said with a grin, "if I put you in any hot water, but I'll call her up at once. All I needed was a few rags for the child I'm treating. Really."

Yet they continued to look at me suspiciously until, in their presence, I had called up the superintendent herself and exonerated them. Of course, the office was spick and span; I have seldom, in fact, seen one so well attended to. The old woman left, followed by the fat man trundling his cleaning trolley, and they went back down the hall, at the far end of which I could now see the figure of a girl escorted by a nun.

The child clung to the wall, slowly fumbling her way down toward my office. Every now and then the nun would gently reach out to steady or support her.

Laura was the same. And a minute or so later she sat beside me in her usual manner—hunched over, eyes looking at the floor a few inches from her feet, one hand indenting her face. There was no noticeable change at all. Only the drip from the nose had ceased.

Although I greeted her warmly, I tried to avoid questions this time in order not to press the issue of an answer. After a while I decided that, since it was a warm day, I would take her out and walk her around the neighborhood; there were months enough ahead when we would be closeted indoors.

It was the slowest stroll I have ever taken. But it turned out to be one of the most exciting.

Block by block I managed with her, aware of the stares of passers-by, the less hidden gawks of children seeing the hunchbacked girl's gait for the first time. I tried to direct our steps past shops, so that I could comment on their windows as we went by.

"Look at all those shoes, Laura, they've just been repaired. And those there lined up, waiting."

SPEEDEE PARKING. A used-clothing store. An evidently derelict Department of Sanitation office, folders of papers dangling uselessly from hooks.

Somebody passed, saying, "Those hoodlums'll . . ."

Scrawled enigmatically on some boarding, LEAVE ALL MERCH WITH MINNESOTA MINING.

"Watch the curb," said a woman to her child.

I wiped my face with my handkerchief. What would happen if this went on—and on, and on? If I never got through to Laura, ever?

"Feeble-minded about money . . ."

"I tell you, it's the pills . . ."

A cop stuffed a manila ticket under a windshield wiper.

You couldn't live on hope forever.

WALK—DONT WALK.

"Kiss me again," she said, and he did.

On the corner where we had crossed was the smell of frankfurters and sauerkraut. Kids were lining up for hot dogs and soda. The vendor had a colored parasol above his cart and a rutted face that I knew, somehow, could only be Italian.

"*Va ben'?*"

"*Non c'è male!*"

I talked to him in dialect a bit and as the line of boys paid—swarming off, I noticed, on screeching roller skates—I ordered a hot dog as well.

"And one for the *piccola* . . . for the little one too?" he asked, with gentleness.

I think at that moment I looked at Laura with a kind of entreaty. Would she never change?

"Like one, Laura? They're good."

"Sure she'd like one," said Cesare, basting his buttery mustard between the well-cooked frankfurter and slit coney bun and handing it to her. She took it at once.

I tried to cover up my observance of this as I paid the Italian vendor, and, munching those delicious sausages, we strolled on, hand in hand. No home cooking could match the taste in my mouth then. I had always loved frankfurters on a street corner.

It was a busy little community we had wandered into. People were passing in and out of small stores, trucks were disgorging cargoes, children out from school went skipping ahead of their parents, newsdealers and candy stalls were doing a thriving business selling five-cent items to the young.

There was one particularly animated group of children on the sidewalk, the girls skipping rope in turns and the boys playing sockball. Vaguely, at the end of the street, I was conscious of the other group on their roller skates. We made our way slowly ahead.

We did so, passing more shops and stores, on many of which I commented, laconically, for my charge. At this point I became aware—as does anyone in a city street—of a climate of aggression building up. The four or five young lotharios on roller skates had cut back behind us now, up a slight incline, and were laughing and yelling together. These fairly harmless exhibitionist youngsters were indulging in a sport of my own youth; they were racing up behind some victim—preferably a girl—on their skates, and emitting some pseudo-Indian war whoop at the last moment, calculated to terrorize their prey. I was cognizant of it occurring two or three times behind our backs as I steered Laura down a side street out of harm.

Suddenly the gang charged around the corner. It was all a moil of adolescent bodies milling down the incline, heady with youth, and cresting the surfaces of the unsure sidewalks with precarious balance. While it was happening, I was thinking fast.

They would pass by us . . . on us. Such was inevitable. But they could hardly vent their extraverted vigor on a virtual cripple like Laura. At the same time, they might wish to give her a shock. And in those fractional instants I was not so certain that this might not be the best thing imaginable for my adopted patient.

I have mentioned that the schizophrenic finds it hard to distinguish between figurative and factual. I have also contended that language is a prime instrument of human development. But I wanted Laura to *imagine*. As the roaring roller skaters advanced, yelling and shouting down that city street, I was happy when she clung to me.

Imagination, linked with perception, is essential for a healthy adaptation to the real world; yet imagination also implies a certain withdrawal into the mind and, as such, can ironically be the source of pathology in the psychotic. Laura was clutching me to her.

Shrieking and screaming, the four or five young roller skaters were upon us. A crescendo was achieved. Laura grabbed my arm!

The boys approached, their skates cutting into the tarmac. "*Look out!*" screamed one.

"We're comin' to get you," cried another.

Laura grabbed my arm. I saw her taut, congested face. Her frightened eyes moved, living. She leaped out of the way, almost adroitly. One arm went around my waist. Very frightened, and still continuing to cry, she held onto me for protection. I had never seen her cry so profusely before, and as she looked up at me in those moments, her tear-streaked face gasping for breath, she must have wondered why it was that I was smiling.

"There's nothing to be scared of, Laura. No one's going to hurt you. Those boys were only playing. They've gone now, see."

As I consoled her, still holding her to me, I knew that I had just seen Laura for the first time—the hidden person inside the shell, the frightened child whose barricade had yielded to me for a second. She had responded like anyone else to a moment of fear. Like anyone else she had reached out for protection. *Laura was not psychotic.*

By the time we re-entered the Institution doors she had regained her usual isolation of demeanor and I felt like singing.

"Did you have a good walk now, Doctor?" asked the nun at the door of my office.

"Yes, Sister, very good, thank you."

"Come, Laura. We'll go back to the dormitory, shall we?"

The nun took her away. I stared out of the window onto the street. But I saw little there. Instead, I saw a lonely girl who had been bitterly abused by life reaching out for the protection of another human being. I could almost feel her arms about me still. My task was to get Laura to develop, and widen, this trust.

When the threat from the outside had increased, as it had with the roller-skating boys, she had abandoned the fortress of her inner world and come out for help. I interpreted this to mean that Laura needed a reason for reaching out as well as someone to reach toward. Deep inside her she *wanted* to be more accessible. Was she at long last beginning to relate to the world about her? Only the months ahead would show. My job was to wait—to wait for Laura to need me again.

12

I had not been wrong. Or perhaps I should say that Sister Paulette had always been right.

Although in the months that followed only the seasons seemed to change, as far as my sessions with Laura went, I sensed a fragile alteration. And there were times when I needed the slightest sign for encouragement.

The girl reverted at once to her usual behavior. Her lack of communication was virtually total. Still and all, I felt her presence, I felt she was reacting, and aware. During the long monologues there were moments when her head would come erect and I would look into her face and establish eye-to-eye contact. I told myself that Laura would always have been the kind of child in whom there was more going on inside than appeared on the surface. I found myself more comfortable with her.

This was apparent in a number of ways. The music of the merry-go-round on my desk caused almost imperceptible reactions on Laura's face, and though she couldn't speak it was somehow as if she were responding to me. In consequence, the words I had to find came more readily somehow. I learned a new language, of a kind. A rhythm, a pattern of communication, was being subtly woven between us.

During our walks outside together, I took Laura through the Institution grounds, where we would spend our time on the swings or the seesaws, which she also liked. The latter activity, in particular, made for rapport since she had to respond to my own balancings. She found neither activity threatening now, and both obviously stimulated sensations within her. For a while it was the closest thing to progress I could muster.

When the weather became too cold to go out we passed our hours together in my office, which had come to resemble more of a playroom by this time. Carefully, one by one, I would bring the toys from the shelves over to my desk, so that they came into her vision without being forced upon her. And I would talk, and talk.

As a matter of fact, I became a bit of a connoisseur of toys in those days. I believe the industry has reached a volume of nearly $3 billion at the manufacturing level, and I had not realized until that period with Laura the standards of verisimilitude it sets. In shop windows I passed that winter I was made aware, thanks to the needs of my patient, of dolls that eat, urinate, dribble, grow teeth, burp, cry "Mama," and sing (a transistor running a record within). Some had removable toenails for the application of polish while others unzipped to produce a baby doll. No self-respecting dolly, moreover, came unprovided with bottles, spoons, pipes for blowing bubbles, soap, tissues, pacifiers, swabs for ear cleaning, and—in one case I noticed—a small enema pear. Let no one say that Miss America is not being prepared to rear her children!

Still, I was again running out of things to do and say with Laura, so that when a large jigsaw puzzle caught my eye I went in and bought it. It consisted of 250 pieces and it kept us going for nearly a month.

The scene depicted was a beautiful one, of a farm with a cozy house and trees, various animals grazing around. It was colorful and attractive, and, as the weeks went by and I began to assemble it in front of Laura, I could talk to my heart's content about the missing pieces I was looking for. And as I searched for these among those remaining in the box, I would watch Laura out of the corner of my eye. I would catch her head coming up, her eyes moving as if trying to help me find the piece too. My work was accomplishing its purpose. I wanted to draw her attention without her being aware of the fact; I wanted to involve her in something outside herself without a direct demand being made upon her.

Already another Christmas was on us. The passages and halls of the Institution began to blaze with decorations, and each time I arrived now it was to the accompaniment of some group of girls practicing their carols. I had been treating Laura for a year, and I had not got very far.

In fact, I came to measure—and shall always remember—my time at the Institution by a series of Christmases there. For the nuns it was a time of intense activity, into which they entered as excitedly as teen-agers. I would come across them unsteady on stepladders, hanging garlands of tinsel in the girls' rooms; or breaking every rule in the Fire Department's book as they rigged up lightbulbs on the tree outside the chapel (their wiring was terrible); or again, and most often, I would see them in the vestibule, where cartons of toys, candy and dolls arrived and where each nun sorted out what belonged to her particular children.

Their ingenuity in decoration, too, was extraordinary; how sensitively they could play up the beauty in everyday things— bowls and brass, pitchers and trays. They never rested until every window had its topiary, each door its wreath, until the candles were all in place, and the glitter balls and reflectors and cornucopias and branches of pine and holly were singing with color at each corner.

Each nun made it a point to get every one of her children at least one thing requested on the child's North Pole list. (And no girl knew that the money for such was begged for on bended knee.) It meant a constant round of shopping and organizing for the sisters, who gift-wrapped each present for their girls and gave each one a separate name, and an individual message of love. Mostly, this work was accomplished in extra late hours at night, or else in the very early morning.

Yet how excited they were about it all, chatting in animated groups of their various plans and presents, their special ideas for decorations. On Christmas Eve the pressure increased to a veritable frenzy as the last-minute details, and impending parties, complicated even further the overloaded daily schedules, into which, of course, the sisters never ceased to fit their regular prayers and masses. It was amazing that they did not collapse from sheer physical exhaustion; but as Sister Margaret came to invite me to the annual Christmas Eve parties, her cheeks were bright and her eyes were shining.

When we walked through the corridors together that year's end, the children were smiling and playing and clearly having the time of their lives. This was, I could see, the nuns' reward, to create happiness in these forgotten and abandoned individuals.

We went into the apartments one by one. The girls rushed up to us, pulling and hugging like Santa's pack itself. We had to stop and have ice cream and cake with them, and listen to their little performance. For each group we visited put on something special—singing a carol, doing a Christmas dance, or presenting, in the more ambitious cases, a holy play, perhaps a nativity scene with a lifelike churchyard creche.

By the time I reached the third apartment I had had enough ice cream and cake to last me for the next five years. But it was impossible to refuse the children, who took as much pride in their food as do adults offering refreshment to guests in their homes at holiday time. The sheer fun generated in these rooms was its own glory. Disaster had characterized the life of every child I saw. It was amazing that they could still smile and play at all.

"Lucy's going through a craze for tomato ketchup," Sister Margaret was explaining at my side as we walked down the corridor again. "I managed to get her some for her ice cream." I remembered the pale face with the ooze of ketchup at one corner of the mouth; I had thought it to be strawberry jam. The nun tugged under her chin at her wimple and put some order in her habit, which was suffering, around the headdress, from the ravages of the children's assaults. "There's Betty, who practically lives on crackers and peanut butter. We try not to deprive the child of a right to develop food tastes. But for the very young ones," she wound up in her abstracted way, "I draw the line at three gum balls a day."

I smiled as we rounded a turn and Sister Margaret added, "Lucy once drank a whole bottle of medicine when my back was turned. I suppose she figured it was more sensible, quicker, than taking a single spoonful a day."

"I'd love to show Laura a really big tree, and watch her eyes light up," I said. "There's a mammoth one at Rockefeller Center this year."

"A fifty-five-foot Vermont balsam," said Sister Margaret softly, and I looked at her. For a second I felt like saying, "Did you order it yourself then?" But she had bent her velvety brows together in a frown. We had come to an open door from which light streamed and singing came. "You are discouraged, Doctor, about Laura?"

"Well, I seem to have developed a very slight reaction from her. In working with that jigsaw puzzle I told you about. As a matter of fact, in the New Year I'm going to buy a model house and put it together with her."

The woman was smiling at me, broadly, confidently. Her hand touched my arm. "Don't worry, Doctor. I know for sure that Laura will soon speak to us."

Then she had passed inside and was being greeted by shouts from the girls. A nun was standing in front of me in the bustling, brightly lit room. We had come to Laura's division.

"Won't you have some ice cream and cake, Doctor?" said Sister Paulette, pulling me forward.

"Oh do, oh do," cried high-pitched voices around my knees.

Automatically I accepted the huge wedge of chocolate ice cream and the veritable brick of white fruitcake placed beside it. One child was tugging at my trousers, wanting to show me the doll's pram she'd been given. Another was pointing out the beauties of her golliwogg doll. But I was only half hearing. My eyes were searching for a missing person.

It was not hard to find Laura, for she was the only one not laughing, playing, running, or singing. She was sitting by herself in a far corner, slowly eating some ice cream.

Excusing myself from Sister Paulette, I crossed the room, still carrying my plate, and approached. She made no move. There was an empty chair beside her and I sat down on it.

"Good, isn't it," I said, plying my spoon in time with hers. "I think this is my very favorite kind of ice cream." She said nothing. I bent my head. "Merry Christmas, Laura," I said.

Her face looked up at mine. Then she went back to eating her ice cream. I noted that the card I had sent her was taped over her bed.

("I like the *green*," some girl was insisting nearby. "But you should see its *coat*.")

I stayed with her some moments, and then I left.

"Merry Christmas," I said again before I went. And once again her strange, scarred face looked into mine.

Across the room Sister Margaret was swooning over a stuffed hippo, in red- and blue-checked gingham, that Santa (i.e., herself) had managed to get into one girl's stocking.

I thanked her and asked, aside, if Laura were going to spend Christmas Day with a volunteer family, as many of the children did. Her smile of commiseration stood in for words. Laura would be staying in the Institution.

"She seems to want it that way, Doctor."

13

As I started my second year with Laura I realized that
technically I had little cause for optimism. At the same
time I did feel something had been accomplished; for a brief
moment, at any rate, I had had a glimpse of the frightened
child behind the veil of silence. Furthermore, I cautioned
myself against expecting too much from her; a hypersensitive
like Laura might well sense my disappointment and withdraw
even further into her world of fantasy. The sensitivity of
patients to the feelings of their therapist is well known, often
uncanny. These were the risks I had to take. And the year
started well.

This was thanks to Build-Eez, the "3-D" construction set I
had mentioned to Sister Margaret.

At each session with Laura I worked on assembling a house
from a large, and complex, assortment of interlocking plastic
bricks. I don't know about my patient, but I was soon lost
in wonder at the ingenuity of this toy as, little by little,
from foundations to roof, a most realistic house grew on my
desk. Altogether it took "us" three months. And I was watching Laura all the time.

I would read the directions aloud slowly, and slowly put
the pieces together, sure that she was growing more and more
absorbed in my handiwork. I did my level best to make it a
joint project, and occasionally her head would lean forward,
her face still covered by her hand. Sitting in her chair, she

watched intently as I placed each block in its proper position. Her eyes seemed mesmerized by the movement of my hand, and from time to time I would try ruses to lure her forward. I would purposely attempt to fit the wrong block in position, or I would drop a piece, and then catch her eyes as she looked toward the floor, following it. There were afternoons when her eyes seemed to wander from my hand to the blueprint I was working from, as if to anticipate the next move before me.

At such moments I longed to invite her to help me, but always I was frightened of going too far, of scaring her away, ever deeper inside herself. Patience was my surest tool.

All the same it was exhilarating to know that I had caught her attention, at least, involving her for almost the first time in the outside world. Moreover, I told myself that the bridge I had begun to create between us was a symbolic one—I was building something she had never had, a house, a home. I felt this game incorporated the basis for the most solid, and safest, relationship I could at this time set up with her. It had to be something totally dependable.

However, I am not an engineer and I soon came to realize, as I wrestled with the highly involved directions, that quite a deal of know-how was assumed in the young by toy-makers of today. There were nights when I had to take those head-cracking directions back with me and do my homework on them before I next saw Laura, in order to be sure that our time would pass smoothly and creatively.

It was a very realistic dwelling indeed. Few human beings could want better. The doors were hinged, the windows opened and shut rather better than my own, and the whole was divided like any typical three-bedroom house. The roof was hinged so that one could lift it back and view everything within. By the time "we" had finished our project it stood a proud foot high, and approximately two and a half feet long.

Next, the tiny kitchen on one side was equipped with every

modern convenience imaginable: refrigerator, stove, coffee percolator in the breakfast nook, and wall-to-wall cabinets.

The afternoon I planned to introduce the toy furniture into the dwelling was a rainy day in March. Before Laura made her long walk down the corridor, half supported by a nun, I sat and brooded over the pieces. And the two caught me at it. Sister, with a smile, set Laura down beside me and I began to talk to her about our problem. My uncertainty must have communicated strongly, loosened her timidity, for something unusual happened.

I have never been a great one for figuring out where furniture looks best anyway, and I've always been amazed at the ease with which women seem to find just the right spot for some sofa or chair. Well, the same problem confronted me here—as to where to distribute the miniature pieces. I began with an "old" armchair, which I put near the fireplace, "blazing" cheerfully with artificial logs. And all at once I felt Laura's attention riveted on me. It was something almost physical. She was totally absorbed. I continued my task, slowly and unsurely, supplementing it with comments and self-questionings.

Unlike the jigsaw puzzle or even the erection of the house, the introduction of the furniture involved choice. Personal taste was at issue. I had just finished grouping some chairs around a table when I felt something brush my wrist. Laura's hand reached out into the house, over mine, and rearranged the furniture.

I shall never forget that moment. I felt my heart leap up, as with co-ordinated hands, firm grasp, and almost shining eyes Laura moved the pieces. Her satisfaction was obvious. Her involvement was total. Within seconds she had rearranged the whole interior. It was as if she had been planning it all in her mind for weeks beforehand.

"Ah," I said, "so that's where they go."

She knew exactly. She had come to help me.

I passed more odds and ends of furnishings toward her. They, too, found their places instantly.

"You're right," I said, "that does look nice there."

It was hard for me to speak steadily. Once more she had left her inner hideaway. And as I watched her so confidently arranging the doll's house, it was as if I were witnessing the movements of her eyes and arms and hands for the very first time, an achievement never accomplished by anyone else. It was the feeling you get when you watch a paralyzed child take his first steps, when an infant first speaks, or recognizes you as a parent in the midst of a group. There is an angel who is said to hover over rooftops and look inside and help those in need, and for a while, to me watching her with bated breath, Laura was that angel. And I was happy and I wanted her to know that I cared for her.

A nun was standing in the door.

"Look," I said proudly, "look what we've done. We've made a home."

"How pretty!"

"Laura put in the furniture."

The sister oohed and aahed politely over our work, and as she took the girl away I gently closed the roof. I was sure Laura eyed it with a last wistful glance. My ugly duckling was now a princess.

It was too soon to be overly optimistic but, as I made my notes, I wrote that this memorable afternoon signified not only the depth of her trust, but perhaps the beginning of her return to reality.

By her obviously thought-out arrangement of the furniture she had evinced a strong interest in the house, and therefore what it stood for. Her need was apparent in this interest, her longing to be part of a home, and a family. I looked in my drawer. Hidden from her was the family—a doll father, a doll mother, and three doll children.

That evening I walked out with a springy step. In the vestibule, girls, just back from school, were playing together, whirling each other around, their skirts swinging under short coats. I watched these wild, intense games for a moment, these faces half feverish with excitement, as I tugged up my scarf and buttoned my coat.

One day Laura, too, I secretly vowed, would be someone. It was thick dark as I strode out. A tangle of lights was visible over Manhattan. Escaping from spumes of cloud, the stars were all at once very bright, their jewels glimmering before the driven clouds closed on them again. Was the long winter over at last?

14

Literally it was, but figuratively it was not. I found no fresh hope blossoming alongside the first flowers.

The week following Laura's "help in the house," as I now called it, she had taken the miniature dolls I produced—mother, father, and all three children—and carefully placed them in the appropriate rooms in the house: the woman in the kitchen, the man seated comfortably in the living room, and the children in the little beds. Through play she was reconstructing a vital part of her life, one she had so tragically missed out on.

Yet after that effort she made no indication of change at all. My own feelings and urgencies had to be most carefully evaluated, I knew, and not allowed to intrude on what this young person most needed from me now, a willingness to endure, the spirit of King Lear's "Pour on":

> No, I will be the pattern of all patience;
> I will say nothing.

For if Laura was to unfold, and grow, it had to be on her own terms, when she felt it was safe. There could be no forcing this sensitive plant. She had to set the pace and I had to be by her side, ready, taking strength from the example of the nuns, whose courage was so radiantly converted into patience.

Apart from that single incident concerning the building of

the house, then, the entire second year of Laura's treatment was uneventful, repetitive. She remained as she always had been, silent. The skies grew more blue, the sun lobbed higher every day. I took her out into the grounds again and swung her through the air, watching her brooding face, her tow-like hair flying out behind the beret some sister had given her that year. The leaves shimmered with heat, the flowers the children tended were crisp with color in their beds, grasshoppers spurted in the paths, but Laura was the same, gripped stiff with intensity, mistrust in every effort she made to get down the passage to my office each visit. The consistency of her movements and attitudes could be, and were, written down in a few sentences; they echoed through the pages of my thickening case folder.

I tried puzzles, games, an inconceivable number of ingenious diversions without stirring the slightest interest in her: Talking Telephones . . . "Wonder" Bubble Games . . . Shapees . . . Baby Crawlalong . . . Race-arama. I got to know the repertoire by heart. She would watch as I worked with these materials, but there was no further participation in anything I did, except occasionally to accept the candy bars I offered her.

Week after week she remained passive, uninvolved except for minor visual interest. And after a while even the more sensational of these activities began to lose their power of drawing her attention. Our walks through the grounds, and neighboring community, were coming to seem routine. The time of each session was starting to stretch out painfully. I began to despair of doing anything for her.

I would search her sad, wan face, so often streaked with tears, and wonder what inner agonies were in bondage there. I tried not to show my strain.

When she came back from camp that fall just the same, and I recommenced our interviews, my hopes grew dimmer still. She even turned her eyes away from the toys and me, to stare at the wall or at her hands. I kept telling myself that her

No Language But a Cry

symptoms were her only way of attempting to alleviate her problems, managing her enormous anxiety. Whatever else the penalty, insulation from the world meant safety, protection from being hurt again. I would tell myself, too, that in therapy everything she did took on excessive emphasis because of the proximity of our relationship and my critical observation of her. With children the treatment process is to some extent an artificial situation, for (among other things) in a group of kids the adult's attention will be focused on the child creating difficulty rather than on the silent loner.

As the weeks went by, I realized I was approaching a third Christmas in the Institution. I had been treating her for two whole years. Yet the passage of time was important. If it was Laura's inner intention to test my endurance, I had to hold on, like the nuns, and pass the test with them. It was, indeed, a challenge. At this stage a psychoanalyst can be likened to a blind man who knows there is a stranger in the room, but does not know in what part. I had to find that person; and to do so, I took strength from memory of the many deprived youngsters I had dealt with, those who had never known the warmth and love of close human relationships, and, in truth, I was urged on by that tenacity established in me by my own childhood, for I had had to overcome strong cultural barriers.

Slowly, as the winter months wore on, I began to sense that the second year of treatment was a reaction. It had been for Laura a moment of untold daring when she had reached for my protection from the sanctuary of her isolation. Perhaps the pain of wanting, the depth of her hunger, were almost more than she could bear during the separations brought about in summer camp, in which I had had no contact with her. Possibly she sensed these separations as a further rejection. Better to go back to the isolation of her inner fortress. Such interpretations are no fantasy. Time after time I have seen children who have been denied solace from their parents literally force themselves to *stop wanting* as their only means of ending such hurts.

The cold days continued. Carols began to fill the halls and rooms. Again I would stumble on some group of nuns in raptures over a doll or toy.

"Who gets the fuzzy bear?" I would hear as I went by.

There was Sister Paulette busy gift-wrapping a simple rocking horse, while a colorful stuffed pig was being eased into a gilt box by another sister, and a wooden mule, with floppy ears, on rollers looked on out of the white-rimmed eyes of some tragic clown—all set for six furlongs around the dormitory, no doubt!

Once more the decorations went up and I realized how Christmas gave the children a sense of security, as well as pleasure, how clever they were in helping with the ornaments, swagging ropes, gilding walnuts, making little popcorn balls, or strings of berries. I passed one room where a nun was helping a tiny, intent dark girl, who was having considerable difficulty with the beak of her dove of peace.

"*Hold* the glue now, Amy, dear, don't drink it."

Another, whom I knew slightly, rushed up to show me her "angel's-hair," a sort of spun-glass halo that seemed to contain all the light in the world. Yet another presented me with the "jewel case" made for her favorite sister; it was simply an old egg carton, but it had been painted with infinite care and endearing clumsiness.

The set pieces in the dormitories were again being meticulously prepared.

"Jane, who do you want to be?" I heard late one afternoon on my way to see the superintendent about something for Laura.

"Thomas," came the distinctly doubting reply.

"Okay, all the disciples over here," the sister could be heard instructing. "Now, you're all meant to be fishing, see."

"Where are the fish?"

"Let go of the net, silly."

"Peter, you're going to have to swim to shore."

This was one Bible story, I felt certain, that had to be a success. Involvement was total.

That year I gave Laura a clown puppet, which I hoped might please her, constructively. The clown had baggy legs and stilts that could articulate amusingly in many directions. I never saw her play with it.

That was the Christmas I identify in my mind now as that of the soap cookies. The Institution was fed from an enormous, medieval kitchen, which I had taken to dropping into for a cup of coffee and a chat with the nun who supervised the place. This was Sister Martha, a stout, cheery woman whose Buddha-like body seemed insecurely imprisoned in her habit. At least three of her chins escaped from her wimple and were nearly always in motion in some chuckle or story. She was a genuine magpie and, giving her that season's greetings, I found her living up to her reputation.

Sister Martha was very proud of her kitchen and she ran it most efficiently. This Christmas, however, calls were coming in from all over the building complaining about the little animal cookies, or cookied animals, she had had made and sent up to the various dormitories. To put it in Sister Margaret's metaphor later, the girls' mouths were not merely watering from the cookies, they were literally blowing bubbles with each bite.

The truth turned out to be that Sister Martha had taken on a substitute chef, a soft-spoken and soft-shoed individual who had conned her into believing him to be a gourmet cook, despite the fact that the last five years of his life had been spent behind the wheel of an oil truck. In the darkened storage room this operator had confused a barrel of soap powder with flour, and all the girls got free bubbles with their Christmas cookies as a result. For months thereafter it became a standard form of greeting to Sister Martha to call out, "These cookies taste of soap." At the time I bade her a merry Christmas they were soap.

Language

During the few days off that followed the festivities Laura's image haunted me. Wherever I was—in a department store, subway, or at home—I seemed to see her scarred face, with the big tears slowly rolling down it, and that motion with which she sometimes turned one willowy wrist this way, and then that.

In those days her eyes seemed my only access to her inner self, and throughout the past year her eyes had started to observe, even squinting, and thus to show the intensity of longing in that bruised soul within.

The new year began. It grew bitterly cold. Children and nuns went about their business behind the massive walls, and on the way back from some visit to the Institution I would hang from a subway strap, rather gloomily contemplating the gaily smiling girl in an ad that informed all and sundry "THE COMPLETE BLONDE HAS EVERYTHING. . . ."

At this time, too, I learned the surprising manner in which children "inside" made surrogate families of their own, composed of their peers. The peer group had an all-important role in the lives of the Institution children. In fact, I would venture to say that the group was of greater significance than the group mother, the nun who acted as actual mother substitute.

The children sought recognition from one another, competed for status, and were at the same time welded by a loyalty that is not often found in the ordinary family. They were extraordinarily perceptive of shortcomings, both physical and mental. The older girls borrowed each other's clothes, helped one another with homework, freely loaned what little money they had, and—all-important!—set each other's hair at night. There were many traumatic moments spent over teasing and back-combing, I am sure, and agonies entailed by a barrette or a bobby pin.

In a family a child can receive recognition from adults, from intellectual achievements, being useful, etc.; the institutional child's identity is closely tied with membership in the peer group. Thus difficulty in making friends was a cardinal problem for a child within the Institution, so much so that there was the danger that excessive individuality or idiosyncrasy tended to be frowned on by peers. The child out of step—loner or oddball—was penalized. There was the danger that variation was simply looked upon as error, a misevaluation very common to our society at large.

Laura suffered intensely in this respect, for she was obviously quite different from her peers. Her despondency and isolation robbed her of all identity, which is largely a sense of importance felt when we are loved and needed. She had no family, no affinity.

Worst of all, the basic tool for human communication was absent, dramatically emphasizing her apartness. Laura's lack of language reduced her to the most primitive level of existence, in which merely physical wants are felt and met. Nor did the printed word, in the stories read to her, trigger its oral counterpart, which so often in turn releases a meaning we seem already to possess. Until I worked with Laura I had not realized how blocked a mute can be.

It was only later, I think, that I appreciated the general amazement among the Institution staff that I had chosen Laura at all. The nuns had more than their share of aggressive, "attention-getting" children who all but exhausted them daily. The child soon got to know that the one who made the loudest noise, and was most disruptive, tended to get the most attention. As in life.

So as I strolled through the passageways now I would find myself taking notice of the girls standing alone, watching the others play. I would see them sucking their thumbs in odd corners, or on the fringes of groups around a nun. And I would stop and talk to them, and try to take an interest in some detail of their lives, knowing that unfortunately I had only moments to give. Still, I felt that if everyone responded in this way to the needy, the crumbs might add up to a cake—even if only to a soap cookie. One never knows what potential can be released in lonely children and one does not have to be a "professional" to lend a helping hand.

During this now declining winter I would meet with the nuns in staff groups and express such feelings. They seemed stunned by my exposition of what to them was the obvious! From me they had expected some technical advice, I suppose, some newfangled "method" for reaching the difficult child, when they knew as well as I did that what was needed was human understanding. As a result, they unbent. In my talks with them I tried not to wrap mental illness in a mystery. In fact, I tried to show how religion and psychology can each enrich the other.

For surely the psychoanalyst and priest both agree that righteousness and decency are precarious concepts. And many of the procedures of contemporary psychotherapy are, it has been well remarked, those of the divines of old. The noted philosopher-theologian Paul Tillich remarked, "Only a priestly man can be a complete psychiatrist." The confessional nature of both creeds, or approaches, has also been observed, and in both, of course, the confession is sacrosanct.

Above all, a person approaches both *in need*. Both psychoanalyst and priest are, essentially, ministers to human suffering; they must have a deep faith in human beings, and a hope for eventual health. Putting such bridges across to the nuns enormously enlarged our dialogue, and they felt more at ease in speaking of the everyday needs of their children. But in the early days of that year I had little notion of any break in the dam of Laura's solitude, let alone any suspicion that we stood on the brink of a raging river of opening emotions.

15

The musical merry-go-round, the doll house, and the doll people who lived in it became the community, the environment in which Laura and I met and spent time together. They provided a constant, and, for the purpose of advancing Laura's security, I wanted her to have this reassuring predictability each visit.

For the most part she spent her time listening to me talk, growing somewhat more attentive as I wove stories about the inhabitants of our doll dwelling. Occasionally, when I posed some conflict in the lives of these little people, I would see her bite her dry underlip or wet it with her tongue. Each conflict I presented was a common familial situation and I could now see the reflections of the surrogate tension, or anxiety, in her face. I knew she felt for the people in the house and I wanted her to observe their occasional frictions while remaining safe herself.

In this way I might help her to manage her emotions more surely. On the whole, however, our make-believe characters, living a part of life Laura herself had only briefly experienced as an infant, expressed warmth and happiness. The doll parents were basically accepting and loving in their attitude to their children, and the security of each of these persons was brought out firmly as they went about their lives indoors.

In short, the picture built up over the weeks was of a normal, healthy family, mature in their responsibilities. This was the frame of reference in which I wanted Laura to compare her own experience, and understand the reactions of others to her. But once again it was slow work.

"How's it going, Doctor?" Sister Margaret asked me one night as our paths crossed on my way out.

I fear I retorted almost snappishly, "All right, but I can't work miracles, you know."

At times the girl seemed wholly absorbed, chin in hand, mouth slightly ajar, listening to my stories and watching the tiny people as I shifted them about the house on various errands. And when I spoke aloud for the doll people she seemed as oblivious to my presence as if I were some puppeteer. They were alive. Her eyes widened and she brought her face closer to the house in order to secure better vision, since, like all squint-eyed people, she was afflicted with double images beyond the point at which her two lines of vision intersected. Her muscles tensed, and in some apprehension I felt that the time had come to take this mimicry a step further. I would re-enact the tragedy of Laura's own life.

That night I passed Abe, the newsstand vendor, with a nod, and made for what had by this time become my favorite friendly neighborhood doll store, where I made some more purchases.

I intended to provoke Laura with a situation akin to that responsible for her present fears and confusions. Together we would plumb the depths of her personal nightmare.

So, while the large doll house I had in my office would serve admirably for the hospital, or, again, the Institution itself, I had to assemble some impersonation of her own home, where the assault on her had taken place. Here my visit to Di Salvio's building, as well as my talks with the Meyers, assisted me, and I was able to put together a plausible mock-up, together with a tiny crib and infant doll. Additional adult dolls, which I myself clad rather clumsily as doctors, nurses, or domestics, helped complete the total background of her life before her admission to the Institution. The scenery was set. The script had already been written. I confess I was on the edge of my seat the afternoon Laura was brought slowly down the hall to see me, to watch the painful re-enaction of her life.

With the usual smile, and sympathetic nod, the nun left her with me. This time Laura watched and listened attentively from the first. Her facial expressions became more mobile, her lip movements restless, her darting eyes evinced strong involvement in what was happening.

I worked slowly. This was something that had to be handled with kid gloves. It is extremely difficult to know how much we remember of our childhood. Furthermore, it is by now fairly well established that the memory protectively buries unhappy experiences for us—at least, many of them. Yet this very lack of tangibility, in the conscious frame of our world, itself generates highly emotional anxieties.

Such apprehension can, of course, reach a really serious sensation of helplessness—like fighting shadows or fencing in dough.

In Laura's case I had to tread as delicately as Agag on the quicksand of her most intimate traumas. By now these were highly generalized. Her anxiety had become so basic that almost anything specific might be perceived as menacing, and trigger off a self-protective response. Truly she was one who feared the world, and once more I held my breath before beginning the final experiment with her fantasies.

Here the profundity of Laura's fears was the issue. Unable to be articulated (due to her lack of speech), they became reinforced within her in a kind of vicious cycle of alarms and anxieties, touching each other off. The difficulty was in herself—she was her own enemy—and as my hands hovered over her miniature home I was counting on the fact that she had fully accepted the doll people into her own world, and developed affinity for them.

"Look, Laura," I said. "Here's the father. He's looking out

the window. There's a fruit store beneath, see, so perhaps he's calling down to his wife to bring up some oranges. Or maybe it's that Italian bakery he wants her to go to. They make such good *cannolos*. . . ."

For a month we lived in Laura's imitation home. As week after week I prolonged the play-acting, prior to choosing my moment with her, I began to see what thoroughly satisfactory companions the make-believe people made for her. They were familiar—with their flesh-colored, well-nigh cherubic faces and realistic clothes—yet far too small to constitute a threat. She could enter and leave their lives unnoticed, and without question. There were no expectations to be fulfilled, and I made sure there was ample opportunity for her imaginatively to experiment with various "safe" situations. Her empathy was never injured. It was like a TV drama, where you could rerun the tape, or stop the slaughter, or prolong the embrace at will. I was banking on a really deep involvement, for each session now we were re-enacting the beginnings of her own life. And at the end of a number of weeks, as she took her place beside my cluttered desk, I began, "And now, Laura, this is the story of a little girl, someone I know. Let's see what happens, shall we?"

The infant doll was in its crib and I made the mother feed it. The cot even rocked a little! Hunger, love, the tactile care of a mother's hands—the role made all these elementary needs most evident. The child wept, slept, crawled, cried.

Then something went wrong. Far from consoling their offspring, the doll parents became irritable, impatient. They punished the child. They did so inconsistently, ranging from moments of care to those of snarling rage.

Laura's eyes glittered. Her whole body tensed, then twisted from one position to another at each new scene I created. Fears flickered on her scarred face like lights on a screen, or shadows on a surface of water. I could tell that her emotions were reaching a peak by the rapidity of her breathing, and I intensified the infant's frustrations as vainly it cried its heart out to its parents.

For me it was our tensest moment together; I was playing on her emotions as another might on a Stradivarius.

Now that she was so rapt I decided I could not let her revert to her protective indifference at the close of the session and be taken back to her "fortress" by the nun. Laura had to go the whole way. I had to get her into the plot.

"Now stop it!" I mimicked for the mother.

"She cries too much," I made the father shout out in a burly voice.

The scene shifted from the infant-mother relationship to the angry struggle between the parents. The father bullied and blustered. The mother responded in kind. Their mutual recriminations built up to a slow fury. Laura's eyes passed from one to the other in a kind of rapt passion; despite her spinal deformity she almost reared up in her chair at what she saw.

The child was crying. The husband thrust his tiny, red doll face forward into his wife's.

"Shut that brat up!"

"Do it yourself!"

She jerked at him, and they exchanged blows. I created a fairly convincing clatter of their furniture, minute cans rattled, together they lurched uncertainly into the bedroom, where, for a second, they stood fairly glowering over the crib.

Laura was standing up.

The parents began beating the child, and as they did so a great strident wail went through my office, and through my being, and as if through the foundations of the Institution itself—"NO! NO! NO!"

Swaying as she stood, eyes wide and face contorted, Laura crushed the mother doll with her right hand, then grabbed it from me with the strength of despair and began pounding it over and over with her fist, at the same time yelling, "No! No! No!"

She was standing panting, breathless, when suddenly in a single move, and with the same feverish strength, she sent the entire two doll houses, and all their contents, crashing to the floor around me. Dolls and doll furniture skittered and scattered about. She was crying hysterically now, balancing her head to keep equilibrium, half stunned in appearance and still shrieking, "No! . . . No!" as I clasped and hugged and held her to me and drew her close and reassured her and held her head against my body, which now she clasped tightly, too, sobs coursing through her chest in spasms and wracking her frail torso.

"It's all right, Laura, it's all right. Don't worry now. . . ."

The nuns came running.

Laura's screams had roused the floor. Their tenor had suggested a child in danger or pain, and at least three worried wimples were thrust around my doorway seconds later. None happened to be sisters I knew, and I realized, as I held Laura to me, that they were frightened that I had been chastising her.

Nor can the sight of the chaotically disordered room, and of Laura's riven face as she clung to me, have done much to disabuse them of their fears. It was several minutes before I could assure them that all was well.

And all was more than well. As I soothed and resettled Laura in her chair, and the nuns rather dubiously left us, my hands must have been literally trembling.

Laura could speak!

This time I at once began talking to her in a different manner from what I had adopted previously. I used the manner of one who expects some response. Come out of your shell, I tried to convey, I know you can.

Trembling all over still, and with face wet with tears, her eyes all dark with pain, she knitted her brows in effort. She was striving to make words come out of her mouth. "You're going to be all right, Laura," I said, "you're going to be fine."

"I hate her," she said, and then, in the same quivering, passionate tone, she repeated over and over, "I hate her, I hate her."

Her eyes were living, but now her mouth was open and from that moist, dazed face words came out. She was no longer mute and those scant accents seemed to me to resound about the space where I sat, flow into the corridors and passageways, and echo through the walls to the sky itself. She had a voice with which to express thoughts and emotions, and truly, in those instants, it was for me the greatest single sound I had ever heard. Together we had succeeded in conquering the silence.

Part Two

LIFE

16

It was nearly an hour before I could bring Laura under control. Alternately sobbing and whimpering, she sat beside me in a veritable jelly of emotions for a while.

Her color was warm, her eyes still reddened with tears. Finally, I succeeded in calming her, and holding her close, walked her back to her room. It was the first time I had done so, but she clung to me trustingly, her silence broken only by a few last tempestuous quiverings.

Sister Paulette was there. A girl getting dressed, or undressed, peeked at us from the protection of a chair.

"Would you stay with her, Sister?" I asked. The nun took Laura from me with concern. I returned to the wreck of my office.

For a second, as I stared at the broken dolls, some smashed beyond recognition, others with missing limbs, I realized how exhausted I felt. Excited, too, but chiefly exhausted. The encounter had taken a lot out of me.

That I was not more immediately elated, or even surprised, at Laura's first manifestation of speech might be ascribed, primarily, to the fact that I was a doctor with a patient rather than a layman with a wounded girl. Not only was I conscious of the long line of if's that lay ahead in Laura's future, but my previous experience with autistic children had familiarized me with their symptoms; it is quite common for such children to remain mute until their emotional state has caught up to a point at which they are what child specialists call "ready" to speak. Furthermore, the word "no" is one frequently provoked since it has been retained as a means of keeping the world at bay.

In any case, the dolls were now dead, the house of little people destroyed. Laura had walked out of it into the world of words.

The phone rang; I identified myself. It was Sister Paulette. "I'm so worried about Laura, Doctor," she said. "I've never seen her like this before. I didn't like to say anything in front of her when you brought her in just now, she's such a knowing child, but she's sleeping now and I did just wonder . . ."

I started to explain what had happened, but checked myself after a moment or two. The nun was immediately overoptimistic.

"Now look, Sister," I said, "I don't want to build up any false hopes. I'm by no means sure that Laura will speak again . . ."

"I'm certain she will," rang back the clear response. "I am going down to thank God for what has happened."

I stared bleakly at the receiver as she hung up. There was a whole slew of harsh realities that counseled considerable caution. Laura's psychic life was still teeming with unknowns, of course. No one could tell how she felt about the past or present. Why, I had had only a fleeting glimpse of her. I began to gather up my notes, put some order in the room. The next twenty-four hours were going to be decisive ones in Laura's short and shattered life.

It must have been a half hour later that I slipped on my coat, took my hat off the hook, and made for the front door. Rounding a corner, three nuns came swirling along. Two I did not know, but the third threw me a pleased smile.

"Hello, Doctor. We've just come back from the chapel," she explained. There was a sense of excitement about the group.

"We've been giving thanks to God," said another, with a knowing nod.

"Yes?" I countered noncommittally.

"For Laura," said the first nun, in the same self-assured manner.

"We're by no means out of the woods with her yet," I managed to get in, but the three were already on their way, chatting contentedly and leaving me staring at the pattern on the tiling. Bush telegraph again. As always, the sisters seemed to know everything almost before it had happened, and I was worried about those added embellishments that always get tacked onto any story as it is passed from one to another—even from nun to nun.

Another was standing before me now. Smiling, her throat firm, and with life fairly pouring from her amused gaze.

"Good evening, Doctor," said Sister Margaret.

It was a curious confrontation in that bare passage, one between religious and scientific belief, I suppose.

"Listen," I began.

"I have just thanked God for the miracle." She gave me a large and confident wink and then passed by or through me, I was in no state to know. Physical obstacles seemed to be easily by-passed by nun-magic. Like Alice, I stumbled out of Wonderland into a cold and sleety winter evening. The gray slab of the building vanished behind me.

When I got home I could not relax. It was distinctly possible that Laura could grow worse, rather than better. The jolt I'd given her had been of such intensity that she well might decide to retreat into her isolation *and never come out again*.

I called the Institution . . . Busy.

I listened to the metronomic regularity of that signal until it all but mesmerized me. Then the switchboard replied. It was Elaine. She put me on to Laura's dormitory at once.

After a moment a shy child answered and, upon infinite

reflection, told me that Sister Paulette was not available. I was breathing deeply. As gently as possible I told the little girl please don't hang up, but press the button once or twice and get me the switchboard again.

"Stitchboard? What's that?"

"The operator, dear."

"Oh, the operator," came the voice in condescension and I could almost hear the childish mind thinking, Well, why don't you say so, then?

Finally, after a lot of searching, Elaine came back with the news that Sister Paulette was in the chapel and couldn't be reached. I thanked her and rang off and started to think.

It was no good rushing things. Laura would need time to recover before she saw me again. Once more I had to remind myself to take her pace, not mine. Shortly before midnight, when the nuns retired, I got Sister Paulette.

"She's still sleeping, Doctor," I was told. I thanked her and hung up. I decided to keep to the normal Clancy "schedule" of appointments with Laura. It would be more reassuring for her to do so. In that way she would not think anything untoward had happened.

A tense week passed. I had to keep myself from the telephone. Would Laura speak again, or would she retreat behind the veil of silence again?

It was a clear windy day when I went out next. Pale clouds scudded fast over the blue of the Bay and the gun-gray bridge I took off the island. Derricks and cables curbed beneath, an occasional sea gull swooping in like a skater, peerless. The moment was imminent. As I bided my time at a traffic light I seemed to feel once more the press of those troubled hands upon me. In all the millions in this city would a world be permitted to come to one of us alone? Or would she be rebuffed once more and turn inside herself, this time perhaps forever?

Entering the great door, I could sense a new atmosphere. It was in a nun's quick look, another's smiling eyes or unusually cheerful greeting. Frankly, their lack of doubt about the outcome was at that moment close to exasperating! I hurried to my office, where I had decided to re-create the playroom that existed when Laura had made her last visit. I put together the remains of the wrecked doll house and set inside what was left of the broken dolls and twisted furniture. In the room's utter stillness the jangling of the telephone had me grasping. . . . It was Sister Paulette.

"Oh, I've been so anxious for you to arrive, Doctor. I'm terribly worried about Laura. She hasn't said a word . . ."

"Not spoken at all?"

"Not a word."

"Are you sure?"

"Positive, Doctor. And all night long she cries . . . worse than ever before."

After we had finished I sat down and reflected, head in hands. So my experiment hadn't paid off. Laura was the same as ever, "worse than ever before." It was all too clear the direction she had taken.

I remember sitting there, hunched over like Laura, when I became dimly aware of two people walking at the far end of the hallway. A nun—and a child. I thought no more about it for a moment, then looked up intently.

Laura was walking toward me unassisted, her pace faster, her balance sure, her feet placed firmly on the floor. She did not lean on the wall for support, nor did the nun (it was not Sister Paulette) have to help her. I stared, entranced. Behind that figure I thought I could see another, a captive child who could barely carry her own weight as she moved.

"Hallo, Laura," I said, as she stood silent in my doorway.

My eyes were on her lips, impatient for some word to come. None did. Instead, in the same frozen silence, she looked questioningly around the room. After what seemed like hours she came in and began to move quietly about, her gaze lingering on individual items. With an anxious look at me the nun left us.

I watched and waited. And waited and watched.

This was Laura's moment. It would reveal the direction of her life. I was on tenterhooks as now she began to touch, and feel over, everything on the shelves, picking up each broken doll and gazing at it wonderingly. Slowly she turned to where I sat at my desk, made an obvious effort of concentration, and said, "Was I . . . in the . . . here before . . . this door . . . room?"

Controlling my elation as I heard these words, I nodded. "Yes."

"Door?" She touched it. "As I remember. Here before. But not sure. Must, must . . . know more. I can't be sure." There was an expression of uncertainty, confusion, on her face as she went on, "I thought so. Things look familiar, more and more. Other things . . . I'm not sure. Where am I?"

Her voice had a full timbre. I explained that she had been coming to see me here for over two years. She sat and listened to me attentively, but didn't respond verbally for a while. I could see that her sensorium was deeply clouded. An analogy might be a drinker's morning-after vagueness, when he asks himself where he is, what he did the previous night.

As to how Laura could speak so relatively adequately after the many years of silence, I can only refer to established clinical experience. An emotionally injured child may show what is called "selective mutism." Who is to know how often such a child talks to itself when alone, with its head, say, under the bedclothes at night? Perhaps that was part of Laura's purpose with the flashlight, symptom of a hidden need. In his *The Nature of Childhood Autism*, Gerald O'Gorman, a well-known specialist on the subject, writes: "Many of the children thus affected obviously understand everything that is said to them, and one knows they could talk perfectly well if they wished to; indeed, from time to time when they are away from interested adults, or when there is no pressure on them, they may come out with perfectly apposite sentences, and then relapse into silence for months or even years."

It should further be borne in mind that, despite visual avoidance, Laura had *listened* for many years. She had attended classes, however passively, and she had heard her peers in the dormitory talking. The understanding of speech involves the same problems as the production of speech. Listening, that is to say, involves no operation not also involved in speaking (for instance, similar loads are placed on memory).

Once again Laura now got up spontaneously, to check and test her reality, walking around the room, touching and feeling toys, books, ashtrays, everything in sight. She was like a blind person beginning to see for the first time. Objects were starting to stand out from the blurred, vague outlines of her previous substitute for reality. Naturally she was experiencing this with some anxiety. Again and again she returned to the doll house and cautiously touched one of the little figures inside.

"Am afraid . . . am I? Am I afraid . . . these dolls?"

As casually as I could I told her that it wasn't the dolls that frightened her, but that they might be like a sort of mirror reflecting events that had hurt her.

She stood staring at the dolls and then continued:

"Why do I cry? I don't know why I cry. Why do I cry? Cry . . . why? It's silly. I'm confused. I cry on the sly. Why? Cloudy . . . why? I've been here . . . cry . . . don't recognize . . . ever . . . I'm *certain*." She turned to me half-pleadingly. "I'm sure I've here before . . . I have, haven't I?"

"You have, Laura."

All at once tears started streaming down her cheeks again. She put a hand to her face and tried to brush them aside.

"There you are . . . cry . . . I don't know what real is any more."

"Come and sit down," I suggested. "Let's talk a little together."

I could see how her very awareness was causing anxieties, uncertainties. This reawakening was going to be crucially hard for Laura, as gradually she strove to orient herself and to induce some logic into the fragmentary chaos of past experience, so well symbolized, as this seemed, by the shattered doll house, with its ruined lives inside.

"I remember . . . people," she said after a while, with a puzzled frown. "Beating, beating . . . a child. Over and over. Beating, hitting. Hitting, hitting. I don't remember what happened after that."

I paused. "You were angry at them for what they were doing, Laura. After all, the child was helpless. And you defended the infant by attacking the ones who were cruel. You punched them with your fist. You smashed them to the ground."

She listened attentively, smudging the tears out of her eyes and turning with a sort of awe to look at the havoc of the doll house once more.

"Did I do that?" she asked.

"Yes, you did," I said. "That's what you did to the dolls and the doll house."

Her tear-bleared face wore a faint smile as again she got up and wandered over to look at them.

"Why do I cry? Why? Cry. They're only dolls. I guess they're not real, at all."

Now we were communicating. That first interview after Laura's recovery of speech was marked by her natural preoccupation for what was real as well as by her fascination for similar-sounding words, or what we sometimes call *clang-association*. Every question she put was basically directed at sorting out reality from fantasy.

She spoke hesitantly, often in clang-association rhymed repetition. She played with words and sentences in a way that sounded well-nigh Joycean. Her speech improved very rapidly.

In fact, linguistically Laura's speech showed a command of words beyond the requirements of stimulus response, or what is sometimes called *input-data*. It was not so much a question of mere vocabulary, but of language properties, the ability to form questions for needs, sort out minor ambiguities, associate and innovate in a creative way. The production of new sentences, based on dissimilar elements of experience involving new linguistic structures, is a capability intimately linked with mature comprehension.

I could not help thinking of Sister Paulette's inner certainties as I listened to Laura talking at this early moment in her perception of reality. She spoke simply yet directly, motivated by a desire to learn about the present and link this meaningfully with the past.

The answers I gave helped brush some of the cobwebs from her mind, but at that stage they could only give dim indications through the darkened passageways of her feelings. At times, indeed, doubt overcame her when she seemed to flounder particularly aimlessly, and I had to extend a verbal hand to help, an equivalent of that arm the nuns had held out to her down the physical corridors of this place. I gave her information about our playroom activities. Vaguely she recalled that I was a doctor, but she couldn't remember my name. Fortunately, children often accept medical facts, and Laura seemed to absorb quite tranquilly the fact that it would take time before she could reconstruct her life and put all the pieces sensibly together.

"I'll be here to help," I assured her, and again she gave the faint smile.

Her very freedom in this room was a new experience. Her movements about it were prompted by curiosity, the desire to learn. She was, in a manner of speaking, introducing herself to herself. Soon she would want to learn more.

Watching her walk about, and investigate, and comment, I

felt a surge of joy. Was this living, perceptive person, more and more firmly anchored in the things around her, the same child who had sat motionless, week after week, month after month, in the chair beside me? This reflection, too, had its corollary: how many thousands of children were there in the world who had never been given the chance to escape from the interlocking grip of their own inner fears?

We had succeeded in opening a door for one such exile. From the night of her fantasy she had stepped into the daylight of reality. There was still a long path ahead, hedged with doubts and uncertainties about her new-won kingdom.

17

A week later I learned that Laura had begun talking to the
other children.

This news, of course, had run through the nuns like a
brush fire, as it had among the girls themselves. Simply
hearing her voice for the first time drew the others to her.
I have already mentioned how the intuition of an institutionalized child can be close to uncanny. There is, after all, a
basic artificiality in their all being collected together in the
way they are.

In this case, the girls' own anxiety about all the unknowns
of their lives was an alliance with Laura's reserve, and helped
tempt her out of it. No one could now say to Laura, "Cat
got your tongue?"

Despite her timidity there were now quick offers of friend-
ship, of candy, and even money (each girl got a tiny weekly
allowance, scraped from charitable donations); there were the
loans of clothes, and—last but not least—of hair-setting lotions
and sprays, a real sign of love if ever there was one. All
this was recounted to me by Sister Paulette.

She sat in my office that February afternoon and talked
her heart out to me. Would Laura get better? Would she
talk more? And so on. I began to sense another side of
saintly Sister Paulette.

"She so needs the love of a mother," I remember her
saying at one point in our conference.

She herself had been this mother, the one person on whom Laura could always depend. Moreover, she had been such unstintingly to a child who was unattractive, demonstrably unrewarding, and unresponsive to attention. It is much easier to love the lovable. Laura was the child who had never laughed or played, and yet I realized that in all the years I had been consulting with Sister Paulette I had never once heard her dwell on her charge's deficiencies, only on her potential for development.

This, then, had been a way of life. The sophisticate might call it "naïve," but in the context of the clear-eyed woman before me it was an immense reverence for human dignity. Through her almost limitless compassion the other-worldly Sister Paulette had developed a wise insight, almost a pre-science, concerning a child's qualities.

Still, this too could come over as a sort of "softness." She was lax on rules and regulations, considered a poor disciplinarian by many of her colleagues, I knew. Each morning without cease she had twenty-five children to take care of, all of whom needed basic help in getting dressed for school or other activities.

"Sometimes," she told me with a wan smile, "I think the superintendent expects me to be a kind of army sergeant. My division has to be spotlessly clean, the rooms orderly, and so forth. I want to do a good job, but I get confused, Doctor, when I lose sight of the individual child in the group. It's not only Laura. It's any single one of them who's upset over a report card, or something of the sort. I'm afraid I'm not a very good leader, I never have been," she concluded, a dejected frown momentarily creasing her lowered forehead. "For me getting the play rehearsal started on time is always going to take second place to the immediate need of one of the girls. Each one is so different, you know."

I reassured her as best I could that we had made a promising start with Laura, and particularly in the matter of language. For it seemed that she was talking well ahead of her inner development, which meant that she had been listening a good deal in those lost years of silence, during the Institution's classes or in gatherings of other girls. At the same time I emphasized that there were a lot of hurdles ahead to leap. We would take them one by one.

Again I touched on the possibility of the recommended spinal operation. At once I sensed that I was talking to one who had grown to know Laura intimately, not by anything she had said, for she had not spoken, but by her manner, velleities in her gait, in short by that communion which arises and exists between two people who have lived close together over many years.

As regards Sister Paulette's conflict between what the Institution expected of her and her own heart, I felt that her inner wisdom needed no support from me. If her feelings as a human being warred against the orders of her superior, this woman, I was sure, would be faithful to herself by giving such duties a highly personalized interpretation. No longer was I deceived by her disarmingly gentle manner, knowing by now that this could mask many a rebel or fighter.

"Doctor," she said, rising to her feet, "you will come to our Day of Recollection, won't you? It's a general day put aside for prayer. We thank God for His mercies. . . ."

She gave me a date in March and I duly noted it on my desk calendar.

As she walked away that afternoon she left me with still more understanding of the extraordinary talent of character, of psychological elasticity, that many of these nuns had had to develop in their special situation. In a strictly circumscribed routine, where there was no place to run away, they had to settle and solve conflicting loyalties, dissatisfied with themselves if in any way they failed to satisfy their superior, yet equally unable not to respond to the suffering of some young individual in their care. This conflict had created in Sister Paulette, at least, an immense spiritual resilience, and a patience that any psychoanalyst could only envy.

Laura was much less easy with me that day. And the following week she was close to edgy. But she talked a little, was repeatedly curious about the playroom (as now I termed it to myself), and in every way showed how vital it was to her to clarify the world about her by sensory perception. I was much impressed by this tactile need, as she touched and felt her way around.

Such was the pattern of the sessions that ensued. Bent not only on clarifying things to herself, but also to me, she became impatient, angered at her own inadequacies. She would even bang my wall, beat her head down on the desk, throw things around the room, yell at me, and cry—healthy symptoms, all.

"Why are you smiling?" she asked in one such moment, enraged.

I explained that thoughts were streaming into her mind faster than she could count, like ponies pouring into a corral, each one unnamed as yet. They were getting ahead of the person sitting on the fence rail and trying to identify them all.

"Take your time, Laura," I counseled repeatedly.

This seemed to make sense to her since gradually her speech became slower as she strove for control over her new verbal world. She was being bombarded by ideas and perceptions streaming haphazardly into her head. Emotionally charged, often conflicting and illogical, this new mental activity required all the energy and effort of someone building a dam against the sudden rage of outbreaking waters. At the same time I did not want her to stifle these important new thoughts; on the contrary, I wanted her to express them individually so that I could help her.

Sure enough, her trust in me increased, and it did so naturally enough since there was so little inside herself that she could hold onto for assistance. It was like the time she had grabbed my arm when terrified by the roller-skating boys. To move the metaphor somewhat, she resembled a child riding a bicycle for the first time, and scared stiff. Now that I had put some training wheels on her bike, she felt confident, in increasing control. In fact, she began enjoying the ride.

In the ensuing weeks Laura began to pick up the fragments of experience and feeling that had branded so deeply into her life. Once more the doll house held her attention, and then came the afternoon when she frowned in concentration at it.

"I keep thinking of a crib . . . and crying . . . I'm a child in the crib asleep . . . other children are crying . . . lots of other children." She turned to me. "I cried all day. Nobody seemed to hear me . . . there's this awful loud noise, and, and something like an earthquake must be, and everything is falling all about me and I'm there trapped in the crib. It happened a long time ago. I always cry."

"Bed, Laura," I said, offering her another association, but at first she shook her head.

Then she said slowly, "I'm shaking . . . a big room with lots of beds. The light from the street helps me see. I see people in the room . . . men coming at me . . . they're going to kill me . . . I hide under the sheet."

She panted in silence beside me for a moment. Then she resumed, "When I turned my flashlight on they went away. . . . They're afraid of light, you see. Sometimes I used to hear them talking to me. They wanted to kill me."

"Why?"

"Because I was bad."

"What did you do?"

"I hit other children . . . I spat at them . . . some woman screaming at me . . . I spat at a child and she took her scissors and said she was going to cut out my tongue."

"What did you tell her, Laura?"

"I cried and ran. Tried to hide under my bed. I held my mouth with my hand and held my lips tightly together. I could see her opening and closing her long shiny scissors as she came toward me." She became more and more frightened as she spoke, tears moved from her eyes, and then she covered her mouth with both hands and collapsed exhausted on the chair next to me.

A crib, a bed, a pair of scissors—what a world of internal terror these ordinary items had aroused in a child alone and unprotected by adults. As she herself put it so simply but eloquently once, "When I cried no one seemed to hear me."

But I could already see that the expression, aloud, of these horror images relieved something of their weight from her mind and I comforted her and told her she was not alone any longer. The light from my desk cast the shadows of my hands on the wall and so, clumsily enough, I contrived to form various animals for her, in the way one often does for children. I made a rabbit and a spider, and a smile stole over her face. After a minute she was imitating my antics, trying to outdo me. The words we spoke in such moments were Laura's link to the outside world, the meaning that life was now having for her. Yet there were times when the effort of bringing painful memories to the surface exhausted her; she grew annoyed, frustrated by herself. Chronic depression over the years had robbed her of humor, which might have helped her to distance, and control, these memories some. Happiness had been an infrequent visitor in Laura's life, and even the pleasant moments always seemed shadowed by some anxiety and fear.

I recall, for example, her telling me about a teddy bear Santa Claus had brought her when she first came to the Institution. The little bear had moved its arms and rolled its eyes and made her laugh. But as Santa's hand approached her face she thought he was going to strangle her.

"Why?"

Laura didn't know. "I was just afraid," she answered dully.

In the hospital days she had heard some nurses holding a child while the doctor "hurt her." The child screamed and all that night Laura stayed awake, an uncontrolled jelly of terror, imagining she was next.

Once when she had dirtied her pants the same person who had threatened to cut out her tongue had forced Laura to eat her own feces. As a result the infant had lived in mortal dread of dirtying herself, to the extent of removing dropped feces from her pants and hiding them under her pillow. Her fears knew no limits.

Such experiences were hard to date or establish with more certainty since her memory was vague, but as far as I could piece them together they seemed to have taken place before she was six. Each flash of memory meant a deepening layer of scar tissue in her sensitivity, her vulnerability increasing as infancy turned into childhood and she was able to identify her loneliness and alienation, and attribute it to herself.

There was the woman with the scissors gleaming between the rows of beds. There was the man with the cigarette whose "evil" face showed in the flickering flame of his match. There was the "mother" who brought her new shoes.

As this kaleidoscope came into some sort of focus for me, I realized that Laura was not too different, emotionally, from when she was two or three. After that time everything that had happened to her was undifferentiated, of the same tone and general color and connotation, namely potential threat causing ever further anxiety and fear. What she had developed was the faculty of shutting herself off at such danger signals, even, of course, to the gift of speech. Now she had to unlearn the intricate patterns of escape she had evolved for herself, no easy task. It would take time for a sense of self to evolve in this mixture of infant, child, and adolescent. At the same time I was convinced, with the nuns, that she had her own unique character. There were moments when I would be surprised by some strange insight she expressed, some striking revelation not often found on the lips of the most sophisticated fifteen-year-old. Her candid sincerity had about it a simplicity that could be quite astonishing.

Laura was developing a mode of expressing herself, of handling her emotions; and as if she knew, all too well, what

No Language But a Cry

she lacked due to her long period of hibernation, she seemed to save and store every new perception jealously, like a squirrel, for future use.

It was in our discussion of her mother that her feelings seemed least stable and contained, and it was in talking of her mother that for the first time since the destruction of the doll house Laura showed me the vast reservoir of her emotions, in surging tides of hatred and self-contempt.

162

18

"I don't know what a mother is," came from the scarred
face of the girl in front of me. "Should I? I know that
each child has one, but I'm different. As a matter of fact,
I don't think I've ever said the word before in my life,
even though I must have heard it lots of times. I do know,"
she went on, as if pondering hard, "I was born from a
mother. Aren't they supposed to be old and gentle and maybe
sometimes fat?" Laura smiled to herself. "They touch you a
lot. You kiss them. They feed you from a bottle, they help
you dress. At least, that's what the girls say. Do you have a
mother?"

"Yes, I do," I said.

"Well, I don't," came the answer, nearly venomously. "What
does that make me then, some kind of a freak? Tell me.
I'm a freak, aren't I? If I weren't, I'd have a mother and a
father, too. Do you have a father? Of course you do.
You see, you don't look like a freak. But I do. I'm ugly.
I'm horrible. If I were pretty I'd have a mother and a father,
wouldn't I?"

She paused, as if groping for words to express all her
sorrow and confusion. Then she went on:

"Nobody wants an ugly child, do they? Look at the mess
of my face. And I've got cross eyes. Take a look at my
legs. Yes, I really can say I don't think I've ever seen anyone
as ugly as me. Have you, Doctor? I am," she said, speaking

each word slowly and with deliberate emphasis, "the—ugliest —child—there—is—here. And that's why I don't have a mother. I used to dream of one, you know. My mother was very beautiful, with long dark hair. She used to bring me presents, those lovely shining shoes. My father . . . well, he was handsome like you. And I was pretty and I lived in a house with a dog, a cat, five fish, a bird and, oh, lots of other animals."

I realized that among the other things Laura had never known was a pet.

"You know," she continued, "I used to look in the face of every woman who came here and wonder what my mother was like. I finally made a picture of her in my own mind. She had a beautiful face and very clear-cut features. Yes, any time I wanted I could see her. I even watched her cook, smile, sing, dance. Oh, she was a very good dancer. We went shopping together. She was so generous and bought me clothes and the prettiest new shoes you ever saw. I love shoes and she always bought me the ones I most wanted. When I was very little they were patent leather with a buckle across the top, and then, when I grew older, she bought me a pair with high heels. I looked so pretty. Then something happened."

Laura frowned. She sank her face onto the knuckles of one hand, as though straining to see into the distance, and the darkness.

"What happened exactly?" I asked.

She shook her head. "I can't explain it. You know . . . I hadn't been well and so . . . I just had to stop imagining her. It was hard to give her up. We'd been so close. I wanted to keep my mother but somehow the picture I'd built up faded, I couldn't get hold of it in my mind, it became harder and harder to remember. I cried for hours trying to think how her hair was combed, or the way she sat, the color of her dress. I couldn't"—Laura hesitated over the word—"*get* her any more. Do you understand?"

"Yes. Go on."

Laura thought for a minute, then continued, "I decided she had to die. That way I'd at least have the memory. So she became ill and died and we had a wonderful funeral, really we did, and I cried so much when I saw her in the coffin. After that it became easier to remember when we were together. A nice feeling. The dead sleep so peacefully, you know. I always thought I would have to wait until I died before I could rest. Yes. That's it. I knew someday I would die, and all the pain would be gone." She paused again. "I look forward to that day."

It had all come streaming out spontaneously. And then I realized that this was as good a time as any to tell Laura what little I knew about her actual parents. I wanted her to know the truth about them, in short the fact that they were in a mental hospital because they could not cope with life and had been unable to provide the love and care Laura had a right to expect. Above all, I had to convey that these people were unable to love—it was not that Laura herself was un-lovable—and this was not easy. How does one explain to a child emotional illness that even adults cannot understand? I started by making the analogy with physical illness.

It seemed to help, but then she said, "It wouldn't have mattered. I would have loved them even if they were sick. Why didn't they love me?"

"They were incapable . . . they couldn't be responsible for anyone, Laura, not even themselves."

"But you can still love a person when your leg hurts, or you have a bad headache. It doesn't make any difference. Leastwise, it doesn't stop you from loving, does it? No. They were sick, and I was something they were ashamed of."

Her thoughts began coursing out in this new direction pell-mell. She spoke almost in a frenzy, and this anger was something I had not entirely anticipated. I could see that basically it was a human wish to arrive at some relationship with others and I was happy to observe this energy. That people might once again become a source of attraction to Laura was what it meant.

To encourage and hasten this development my approach had to be a questioning, a challenging of her motives for still holding herself apart from others at this time, when there were so many around willing to relate to her. While her withdrawal as a child might have been appropriate to the dreadful experiences she had had, the pattern of behavior had to cease one day, if she was ever to come to terms with the world of reality.

But she was still unable to take the hand held out by all those who cared for her in the Institution. This damaged ability to give and receive love acted as the central block to her maturity. Emotional deprivation had formed this hard crust, or carapace, of mistrust; it would be a long time before it could be sloughed off enough so that she could reach out for others. Nonetheless, the first signs, the first glimmers of desire, were evident, and to encourage them I would sometimes play the devil's advocate in our sessions together, even to the extent of being deliberately provocative.

Her idealized fantasy image of her parents was her stumbling block here, as she masochistically blamed herself for the indifference of others. Her ugliness seemed the indisputable premise on which she built the benevolent picture of her parents, her unworthiness for love, and the basic source of her misery. Punishment was her just dessert for her crime of being ugly.

Within this ugly-duckling syndrome Laura had all the logic of some prosecuting attorney. No one, she argued, could be expected to love someone who was ugly. The more she ruminated over this the stronger her self-hatred became. This culminated in frequent outbursts of tears and, one afternoon, in the moment when she held up a mirror before her face in my office, yelling (in perhaps a practiced way), "Mirror, mirror on the wall, I am the ugliest of them all!"

She was annoyed when I questioned her premises here,

and became increasingly firmly entrenched in the conviction that her parents did only what any other parents would do if they had a child as ugly as herself.

Once she stated flatly, "What choice did they have? I would do the same if my child were *that* ugly."

This self-punitive nucleus nullified her inner energy; her strength was always buried under the tonnage of outer disappointment as well as internal fear. The emotional compromise made by Laura was like the gray that results from the mixing of black and white. After you have mingled them it becomes extremely difficult, if not impossible, to separate them again.

Laura's lack of interest in herself, her clothes, her general appearance, her isolation (even the symbolic death evidenced by her mutism) were at this time something she had to cling to. I had found a somewhat similar state in a patient afflicted with obesity. In both cases disappointment with the self supplied the motivating force for suspended animation, a reduction of commitment with life and its problems. Certainly Laura had built up a great case against herself; any disappointment could easily be rationalized as something she deserved. So in this sense there was no longer anything to be afraid of outside since she agreed and aligned herself with the forces in her environment that had been depriving and punitive. In the crime of ugliness she was judge, jury, and executioner. Not to mention victim.

By this time I had come to realize that Laura's personality was, however, a fabric loosely held together, as if with spit and glue. There were but soft boundaries between self and reality, conscious and unconscious, while the individual fragments of this quilt-like fabric were discrete, autonomous, and often plain contradictory. Her positive feelings toward me were intermixed with a childlike negativism or opposition. Symbolically, of course, I stood for all the parents she had ever known, some of whom carried scissors and were trying to cut out her tongue.

Throughout this period, however, she was a good patient and never broke an appointment. Often enough, now, she arrived a quarter hour ahead of time. She was much neater in appearance. Her hair was combed, her clothes ironed and matching in color. Her hanging head and drooping arms were memories of the past. Though on shaky grounds when involving herself in groups, she could now struggle through many a smile or a brief chat with another child. Chiefly her curved back remained as a constant reminder of her personal sense of deformity. At least, of her physical deformity. Her intellectual retardation was something else again.

In common with other girls, Laura had been attending daily classes inside the Institution. No one ever really expected her to do anything in these, but at least her attendance relieved a sister from being with her personally. As the years had gone by Laura had kept up with her class, moving from one grade to another simply on the basis that she was older. Also it disturbed her less to be in the same group. Frankly, as far as the schooling was concerned, it didn't matter much if she sat in fourth grade or seventh, since she wasn't particularly interested in any aspect of life. The classes were mere chronological markers in her days.

I was not surprised, when checking with Sister Margaret, to find that every psychometric evaluation attempted led the psychologist to suspect mental deficiency.

The judging of intellectual skills by testing is a controversial matter, and I was thoroughly convinced that Laura was not defective. Now her new vocabulary and expressive handling of language gave evidence of a brightness undaunted by her traumatic experiences. Whether or not she could demonstrate her skills on a test depended on factors completely unrelated to her intelligence. It was more a matter of emotional stability. I knew Laura well enough by now to realize that subconsciously for her a test situation would represent a mere exercise in self-destruction. Consequently, the day she mentioned to me her desire to be a baby nurse was a red-letter occasion.

Evidently the thought of someday becoming a nurse had occurred to Laura in watching the nuns care for the two- and three-year-olds. She had a feeling that she, too, could help them, and a notion that they might like her.

This interest was charged with personal meaning. It was a real step forward. Here was something useful she could do for others, and, in this case, for those who would depend on her uncritically, without question. It must have been a crucial moment in her young mind when it sought out some protective niche in the world, a first place that might give her a small feeling of importance and recognition without threatening her with inadequacy and competition. Helpless infants love blindly, and with sincere devotion. This—Laura's subconscious must have said to her—was what she would receive, and within the safety of this role she would be free to give what she had.

However, the opposing feelings that any such hope in her mind generated soon came boiling to the surface, and no sooner had she expressed confidence in her idea to me than she started to doubt it.

"What if I should make a mess of the whole thing? Oh, I could never . . ."

Her confidence soon oozed like air from a punctured balloon, leaving her feeling more dejected than ever. The children would never accept her. She was too ugly, etc.

By this time, of course, I had become accustomed to these swings in her emotions. The reaction was predictable, since her ugliness had in those days become a veritable obsession, the focal point of all her uncertainties. She hinged every past rejection, as well as her isolation and self-hatred, on it.

It was a psychological excuse, an "out." After all, any self-concept is better than none and, as in the case of my other patient's obesity, Laura's ugliness represented something to fall back on when things became too tough. So, too, her mutism had been subconsciously an excuse, something to hide behind and a tangible, overt way of showing the world that she was to be pitied and excused from living.

What deeper fears might swarm up in Laura if she did not have this protective cove in which to hide when the seas of life became too stormy? Was she in any way ready to make a more direct confrontation with life? Was this her last line of defense against total self-destruction? I felt certain, in any case, that she needed some defense for her so vulnerable ego and tattered self-image—it was no less, in her case, than the preservation of sanity. So there was a real possibility that improving Laura's appearance, removing the crutch on which she leaned so heavily, could throw her back into the abyss of emotional illness, from which she was so painfully struggling.

On the other side of the coin stood Laura's pronounced progress, and her obvious willingness to fight when the chips were down. The interest in nursing was an interest in the future. Here her spirit had fluttered bravely. I approached Sister Margaret with a plan to have a series of operations performed to improve Laura's eyes, her back, legs, and finally the scars on her face. We decided that the idea could only be put to Laura gradually—seriatim, as it were—and in our next meeting I tried out the idea of getting her to go along with a correction of her strabismus.

It was extremely tricky, to say the least. Laura's basic identity as a person was intricately linked to her body image. Of course, this is somewhat true of all of us, but Laura immediately wondered what she would feel if her body was changed.

"Would I know who I am?" she said. "I mean, would I recognize myself in the mirror? It would be like being born again, wouldn't it?" I was searching her face for signs that would indicate the depth of her fears, but after a while I was happy to realize that I was only experiencing my own anxiety about her situation. Finally, she said, "I think I like the idea. . . ."

This was another important moment in her development. Not only, of course, did we need her full co-operation for such an operation, but her willingness to change, take a risk, was a most rewarding sign of confidence in those days when all of us around Laura were still clutching at straws.

I sought out Sister Margaret at once. Little did I know what a lesson in human manipulation I was soon to learn.

19

Four operations. To face the surgeon's knife once is more than enough for most human beings.

In fact, the first day I'd put my plan to Sister Margaret I had small confidence it would ever go through. Apart from the considerable expense involved—the Institution had no funds to support such surgery—Laura needed an understanding doctor, one who would realize the significance of her deformity. It was not long before I found I had grossly underestimated soft-faced Sister Margaret's determination and surefootedness in getting things done.

Modern cities are wrapped in myriad skeins of red tape; to these the Institution was as subject as any single one of us. Mrs. Clancy's chaotic office, on the afternoon when I developed my idea to the pair of them, was itself a stirring testimonial to such.

Now it was true that any city hospital could have performed this first operation, that of straightening Laura's eyes, a stitching that did not involve the eyeball, only the muscles on either side of the eye. But "any" hospital would not, in this case, do. The impersonal atmosphere, the waiting, the coldly efficient treatment would not have helped Laura emotionally at all in this first step on a journey to a new image of herself.

Sitting on a discarded carton, Sister Margaret sensed this at once and took to the task like a quarterback racing around the opposition and heading straight for a touchdown. As a matter of fact, as a tribute to her determination to get things done, I nicknamed her the "Quarterback."

She immediately called up Sister Paulette, who was not easily traceable at that moment. We eventually located her upstairs. It seemed she had just been summoned to the superintendent concerning a coming command performance for the place, namely a visit by the mother superior of the order. I think the superintendent had been trying to instill more army sergeant tactics in "permissive" Sister Paulette, for the nun came in to us looking thoroughly anxious and distraught. But her mien changed as soon as Sister Margaret mentioned Laura, and all three pitched in to the problem at hand.

As the two nuns talked, and Mrs. Clancy plugged her mobile mouth with cigarette after cigarette, I became more and more bemused. Apparently they "decided" that the operation would be done privately.

"Who's going to pay for all this?" I interjected at one point.

"I'm sure I can persuade some nice doctor to donate his services," Sister Margaret replied.

I laughed. "What if you can't?"

The two nuns exchanged puzzled glances. Well, somehow they would find the money to pay for it. I wasn't to worry. Apparently they planned on calling a nun who was an administrator of a hospital to see if she would allow the use of an operating room and provide a place in which Laura could recuperate.

They chattered calmly on about the various nuns they knew, trying to determine the best way of getting one or the other of them into their little scheme. I listened. As it evolved, the plan outlined seemed to incorporate an intricate maze of telephone calls, personal visits, and not a little outright hypnotism. I left that day shaking my head.

The postscript was awaiting me the following week.

"Oh yes, doctor," I heard in Sister Margaret's mellifluous tones over the Institution telephone, "it's all arranged."

It was? As the nun prattled on, I realized that she had everything ready: a specialist, a hospital, a private room, and a date for Laura to be examined prior to the operation. No experienced social secretary, with nothing else to do with her time, could have done any better. Probably not as well.

Before the Quarterback hung up I innocently inquired, "How on earth did you manage all this, Sister?"

There was a smile in the voice that replied, "Oh, we had God's help."

Such was my first lesson in "nunsistence," or persistence by nuns. It was more. It was an incredible ability to overlook something so out of place as a mere refusal plus an unshakable belief that, if you can manage your way past a doctor's impersonal nurse, and slowly chip away for a while at his indifferent façade, you will reach his sympathetic heart—and that's when you've *got him!* The eye specialist was the first, but by no means the last, of their victims.

Second, I was to learn that Sister Margaret had not followed protocol in the matter. She had failed to inform her senior, i.e., the superintendent, of the project. I could well understand her reluctance, since the whole maneuver was highly devious and out of order. She could hardly bounce into the superintendent's office and announce that she'd just conned half a dozen professional people, and a hospital or so, into helping Laura.

No one in fact knew just what Sister Margaret told that doctor, or what pressure she brought to bear on him. Frankly, I pitied the poor fellow. What chance did he have against this soft-spoken woman, with her clasped hands, her immaculate habit, angelic smile, and Biblical language? He probably never knew what hit him.

For underneath that quiet, ingratiating exterior beat the heart of a shrewd, enterprising, and gifted individual who could size people up after five minutes' conversation. In addition, her training as a psychiatric social worker married with this unusual intelligence to make her arsenal of persuasive weapons most impressive.

Sister Margaret's motives were conspicuously simple. Her cause was children. Like all of us working there, she detested any discrimination against individuals, particularly the poor and helpless. Laura could not defend herself, and so the challenge I had set her had sparked off her full array of talents. Children were her weakness, the torch that ignited all her energy, as she fought to break the vicious cycle of deprivation that besets the parentless. There was nothing dramatic or exhibitionist about this. It was simply a way of life, one of the reasons for her existence.

Since that day I have seen many individuals in institutions become hardened and deaf to the needs of children, people who simply regard themselves as getting through another job. I have seen the rules and procedures, the impersonal bureaucracy of these places, used as excuses to keep from getting involved with some particularly troubled child.

Luckily for Laura, Mrs. Clancy, ceaselessly replenishing her inky coffee, was cut from the same cloth as those sisters in front of me. She was perhaps not quite as clever, nor did she have the advantage of a disarming habit. She was frank and open and did not mince her words, yet there wasn't a child who didn't come to know and love her. She had a great capacity for giving. I have seen her quiet temper tantrums while on the phone to some august city or state official concerning the particular needs of some child. She despised the role of inquisitor that bureaucracy tried to impose on her; rather, she communicated a dignity, a warmth, and a real respect for the children. When she was crossed, however, it was strictly every man for himself.

And so, sure enough, in front of my baffled, half-disbelieving eyes, it came to pass that on the appointed day Laura left the Institution carrying a small bag and escorted by Mrs. Clancy. I saw her off, on that windy street, as I had promised to. The day before she had been frightened, as any child might be by the prospect, but nevertheless determined to go on. My own concern centered on her memory of a doctor hurting a child; I hoped this would not be rekindled by the conditions of the operation. But she seemed calm as she got into the taxicab, almost too calm perhaps. She waved good-bye to me once, and then looked ahead.

The uncertain hours of our gamble were anxious ones for those of us associated closely with Laura. I know we all wished time would hasten its pace the next day, and I for one was on the telephone repeatedly to the hospital.

Finally, I could walk to Sister Margaret's office and give her and Mrs. Clancy the good news that the operation had been a complete success. Laura was being brought back to us shortly. Mrs. Clancy even gave a hoarse cheer.

Laura came back with bandages around her eyes, but in good spirits. I went to see her at once. She was sitting by her bed, impatiently awaiting the moment when she could remove the bandages and see her "new" eyes. I saw no signs of unusual reaction. Her mind was taken up with stories about her various visitors, the cards she had had read out to her from the nuns and the children, and the flowers she had been sent there. These had been the gift of her own group, each child chipping in some of her personal pocket money, and they had meant a lot to Laura. She chattered on, describing the beautiful room in the hospital, which she had shared with another child, and I had difficulty getting a few words in.

As I made my way home that evening, I realized that, however she looked, Laura knew she had played her part. She had followed my directions, summoned up her courage, and come out of her withdrawal. She had taken her risk. It was now up to me to give her what I had promised, or at least hinted at.

20

When Laura's bandages were removed she hurried to view her eyes in every mirror she could find. She was happy with, and smiled at, her new appearance. It was something tangible by which she could raise her self-esteem and begin to direct more energy into living. I had not myself quite bargained, however, on the delight with which the transformation would be greeted by Laura's peers. The girls poured all over her, flattering and congratulating. They seemed particularly to enjoy fixing her hair, combing it and trying every conceivable—and some inconceivable—latest style.

Laura sat there like a puppy while all the attention streamed over her. Yet whenever an adult complimented her she turned her face away and blushed. It was still difficult for her to deal with the flattery or affection of older people. Large doses of either threw her into embarrassment, usually forcing her to withdraw from the situation.

Of course, Laura's converging vision had in the past plagued her with double images and other attendant distortions of the world around her. It had been difficult enough for her to distinguish between reality and fantasy, without having this unlucky confusion compounded with her woes. Indeed, I had often reflected on what an ironic twist to her inner misfortune her strabismus had been. Now everything beyond a few feet was clear, sharp, and distinct. She could trust the images that struck her retina and entered her brain as accurate representations of the external world; and as she repeatedly commented to me on how "different" objects looked to her, I could see that this certainty in her sight was lending her a new stability. But the process of giving a meaning to her experiences was still a laborious, uncertain, and undoubtedly painful process ahead.

All the same, our talks now took on a different character. The frightened turtle, so quick to pull into her shell at the first sign of danger, had risked sticking out her head, and so far so good. The door on the past was gently closing. I pressed home the theme of her ambition to become a nurse. At once she told me how deficient she was educationally, that she would never be able to pass the examinations, and so forth.

"You have to be patient, Laura," I counseled.

The indignation with which she greeted this request made me realize that Laura was in danger of expecting me to be some sort of magician. An anticipation that the therapist, like a parent, is all-powerful and protective is natural enough in relationships of this nature. Here, in this case, it was for Laura as if she had done her part—now what about mine! Moreover, she had been making a lot of invidious comparisons between herself and the other girls while listening to their recitals of personal accomplishments. I began to see that it would be just as well for Laura to understand as soon as possible that I could not be expected to supply her with all the things she needed.

The organization of the Institution was such that nearly every child was given a chance to show some individual talent or skill, something that gave recognition in the group to which she belonged. It might be cooking, dress-making, or some particular aptitude in class—a flair for math, say, or a gift for some foreign language. Stout Sister Martha in the kitchen was unsparing of her encouragement in "home economics."

But Laura was unwilling to cook, or try making dresses,

and had absolutely no interest in boys. In school there would be too many other girls who would be "smarter," who could read and write way above anything she could yet achieve. So I fed Laura's feeling that helping the very young children would reward her without involving her in painful competition, and one sunny afternoon I discussed the problem with our Quarterback. A steaming mug of coffee on a loaded PENDING tray told me that Mrs. Clancy was not far off.

"Laura needs a sense of being of use," I explained. "Accomplishment. It's vitally important to her. I feel certain that if we could assign her as helper to one of the sisters who takes care of the very young children . . ."

"The two- and three-year-olds, Doctor?" asked Sister Margaret. "It's true, Sister Jean is certainly short-handed."

"I'm sure she'd do her best to succeed," I said.

"And what if she fails?" came a rasping voice; Mrs. Clancy strode around the door, several sheaves of leaking files in her hands.

"She won't fail," said Sister Margaret after a moment. Then she looked up at me. "Will she doctor?"

I felt like answering, Not if you say she won't.

"I don't think so," was what I said.

I explained to the two women that Laura now needed a chance to test herself against life, to work hard at something real by herself, and prove to herself something no amount of talk could ever convince her of. Here was a perfect situation, since the chances of her being rebuffed were minimal.

"It's a risk, I agree," I concluded, "but then anything with Laura has to be."

I was watching them closely, for I had yet one more request to make.

Once more the challenge did the trick. The Quarterback went into action and within the hour it was all set up: the job would require three hours' work a day in helping the children dress, playing with and controlling them, and supervising their supper. The age range was two to five. There were twelve in the group. Sister Jean would be pleased to see me about it any time. I decided to make my final pitch.

"I'd like Laura to be paid for her work, if possible," I said.

This threw them for a loop. Sister Margaret politely outlined the innumerable procedures that would be involved in fulfilling such a request, not to mention the other hurdles involving the superintendent's permission, the various signed vouchers, the Labor Department's approval, the okay from the Accounting Department, the Department of Social Services, the Compensation Board, the several other bodies.

Mrs. Clancy then pitched in. If Laura was given a penny, not a cent of Department of Welfare money could be used in her care.

"We happen to be having a visit shortly from our mother superior," Sister Margaret kindly reminded me. "In case you didn't know, Doctor, she is in charge of all the nuns in this order on the eastern seaboard."

"Why do you want Laura to be paid?" Mrs. Clancy asked.

I did the best I could to answer logically. My own feeling was that I saw no use in her doing a job just to keep her fingers busy, any more than I could ever understand why they have patients in mental hospitals doing basket-weaving. Laura wanted to perform a job like anyone else. The ladies we called matrons—lay people who came in to help with the cleaning—were paid, and an observant child knew they were paid. If Laura was ever going to live outside the Institution, she would have to work to support herself and learn the value of money. I wanted her to experience the world of work in all its reality, its demands as well as compensations. Laura knew next to nothing about money as a reality. Her weekly allowance of one dollar had been put into a savings account. The Institution took care of her limited needs.

Sister Margaret listened patiently. "Hmm," she said finally. "It's a good thing God is with us, Doctor. You're giving us such difficult problems to solve."

"Do you think you can get a salary for her then?" I asked.

"I don't know," came the firm reply. "But I'll pray and see what happens."

Somehow I had the feeling that all the time I had been talking she had been figuring out some way of cutting through the red tape that surrounded our lives. It was just the sort of challenge she enjoyed.

A week later I got a call in my office. It was Sister Margaret. She told me Laura would be paid.

"You fixed it already? Wonderful." And then I joked, "You must have a hot line to God."

"No," came back the answer evenly, "but His switchboard operator is a friend of mine."

The best I could determine from her about the complicated manipulations she had performed was that Laura had been placed under "Miscellaneous." The nun in charge of auditing, or accounting, or something had somehow been bamboozled into classifying Laura as such. There was no other way to effect the payment, it seemed. When I cautioned Sister Margaret on taking too many chances on my behalf and getting caught, she came back cheerfully, "Oh, they can't fire us. Where else would they get such cheap labor?"

I thanked the sister and when Laura came in talked to her at once about the job. Her quick smile told me how she felt. She had been accepted and, as I outlined the responsibility of the job to her, careful not to scare her with it, I realized that for me Laura was a mixture of infant, child, and adolescent all in one. I was never entirely certain to which I was talking. But the next week she was working with the children under Sister Jean. The year was going well.

At first a trifle confused about details Sister Jean told

her, Laura soon came to grips with the new routine. The children grew increasingly fond of her as she sat and played with them, or fed them individually.

When I visited Laura two weeks later, they were hanging on her, competing for her attention, calling out her name and begging to sit on her lap. Laura was very busy indeed and seemed to be enjoying every moment. There was color in her face, her movements were alert, her speech spontaneous. She seemed thoroughly wrapped up in the needs of her new charges. At one point, I recall, she looked up and remarked to me, "Oh, I'm afraid I couldn't possibly speak to you at the moment. I'm much too busy."

It was a pleasure, of course, to see her so outside herself, and an added pleasure when Sister Jean came bustling up to ask me to promise that she could keep Laura.

"She has such patience with the young ones," said the overworked nun in charge of this group, "such energy, too. All the children like her."

Laura sensed her accomplishment, and so of course did the sisters. It was "Laura's way with the children." Three weeks and she was almost a professional.

All this was immensely gratifying for those of us who cared for her. It was the first challenge that reality had thrown in her path, and she had done more than merely survive. Life outside her shell had become meaningful, rewarding.

She took to describing to me her thoughts about the children and her new work. Each day now she looked forward to the next as if something better lay ahead with each passing hour, indeed with every minute. The more involved she became with her work the firmer grew the barrier between her past life and her present. She walked with more confidence, there was a new strength in her limbs, a vibrating personality that we all noticed and acknowledged.

The next stage in Laura's vocational interest—and well she knew it—was entry into high school. By now she had talked with many of the other girls going out into the community schools around.

After reviewing Laura's elementary school record within the Institution, the authorities of the high school we approached asked for a psychological evaluation; they were uncertain about her ability to manage the program.

Now the group tests periodically administered in elementary schools showed Laura to be a defective individual. The teacher's report from the fifth grade stated flatly, "This child belongs in a hospital, not a classroom. She is uneducable." It was quite clear to me that the high school would not take Laura if they had any choice in the matter.

Moreover, I feared for her future. It is a very difficult problem in our society to get back on your feet once you have had even an emotional breakdown. Psychological tagging has a habit of sticking with an individual. (We have all heard—perhaps used—the expression, "Oh, So-and-So's been in and out of institutions.") Employers are skeptical about hiring, Civil Service jobs become impossible to get, society as a whole seems to act as if the person concerned has some contagious disease.

The agency psychologist who examined Laura found her intellectual functioning to be well above her previous level, with definite indications that she was capable of at least average ability. It was apparent that at this point she had more of her basic intelligence available for adapting than ever before. As it was, then, everybody crossed their fingers, swallowed hard, and Laura was scheduled to enter high school at start of classes in the fall.

To say that this was to be an important event for Laura would be a wild understatement. It was simply going to demand every atom of her courage, since the situation was fraught with all the anxieties and fears that flooded her in any novel circumstance. Laura was well aware of the problem. She once asked me if the time would ever come when she would be able to have any experience that did not carry its penalty of fear and uncertainty with it. I tried to make her see that in some way it was the same for all of us; it helped Laura to know that we all have to deal with anxiety, and that in this respect she wasn't so different from most people.

But most people don't experience the invigilation of a gimlet-eyed mother superior, and this good woman's visit was now scheduled for an hour when Laura would be looking after Sister Jean's rambunctious children. Would she make the grade? Of course, I did everything I could to give her encouragement; and all our allies in the superintendent's office had it set up to sidetrack the holy mother and keep her interested in other elements of the Institution than the bawling two- and three-year-olds. But, if Laura ever does, I am quite sure *I* will never forget that fatal inspection.

The mother superior, a kind of visiting general for the nuns, turned out to be an impressively berobed and stern-looking woman of some sixty years and some six feet in height, with bulk to match. Alongside Sister Margaret I got caught up in the cortege, which we were determined to steer clear of Sister Jean's domain. At the crucial spot we all, like a practiced platoon of West Pointers, made the same precision turn and led off in the opposite direction, with Sister Margaret whispering away to the superintendent. After a second the latter nodded and said, "Perhaps, Mother, you would care to see one of our classes. We have a fine young biology teacher with a master's degree. From what I understand she teaches in the 'new-curriculum' manner."

This was Sister Philomene, whom I had last seen getting into a limousine one rainy night in Manhattan. And as we approached that classroom where she was reputed to bring Bio III "alive," we were greeted by a chorus of yells, screams, the banging of chairs, and finally a farther door flung open with a nun's head peering out: "Mercy! Is someone hurt?"

I got to open the classroom door first. Sister Philomene

stood firm at the head of her riotous class and as we entered she called out loudly, "First row! To the third row, *advance!*"

It was certainly the oddest classroom order I had ever heard. But like some squad of soldiers, the first row of girls duly moved to the third row behind—where chaos had come again.

A girl with dark hair and a very pale face was stretched back across her desk, gibbering with fright and making plucking motions at her bow. The rest of the class made frenzied grabs at it, too, until I stepped forward to assist. A baby alligator had attached itself to the bow. I gave the reptile a few sharp taps on the head, managed to detach it, and carried it by the tail to the front of the room, navigating overturned chairs and desks en route. Sister Philomene accepted it with a calm and grateful smile, dropping it in one of the little black pocketbooks nuns wear at their waists. As she did so I realized she had no idea it was the mother superior who was visiting her class. And this good woman now looked extremely apprehensive.

Yet the lesson proceeded and, barring one escaped frog, concluded without further incident. At the end of it the girls came up one by one with cupped or folded hands and dropped whatever it was they were holding into the commodious black pocketbook before filing out. I saw more than one lizard go in.

The little nun was totally unruffled. It was evidently all routine for her, and she prattled happily away to the mother superior about the escaped alligator as if the animal were some old friend; she then went into a long story about one of her favorite lizards that had darted into a radiator grating only the morning before. Lizards were *precious*, she wanted to emphasize; it had taken many minutes and a strong screwdriver to get the grating grille off and recapture that lively reptile with the aid of the other girls. "It's a miracle it didn't get burned," she concluded, with a shake of her headdress. "Would you care to see it?"

"I don't believe that will be necessary at this time, Sister," hastily interposed the superintendent, and the mother superior led the way out. It appeared that she did not wish to see anything further that day.

I walked back with Sister Margaret.

"Oh, that class demonstration was nothing to what goes on in Sister Philomene's room," she assured me spiritedly. "She has fish tanks up there, lizard tanks, at least half a dozen alligators, and goodness knows how many white mice, frogs, hamsters, and the like. No cleaning woman will go near the place. Why, do you know, she used to lend out her animals to the children like a library lends out books? We had to threaten practically to hang her unless she stopped the practice."

From which our talk turned to Laura. She had been saved the ordeal of "inspection" for a day at least. And what a long way she had come in her struggle to survive. Neither of us wanted to show the other quite how worried we were about her forthcoming entry into high school. However hard Laura worked, there would be so many basic skills lacking, which she had never had a chance to develop. If she failed here, there would be another scar on her thinking process, making eventual success more distant. We were both intensely anxious about that fall.

21

It came soon enough, with its clusters of children around candy stores and stationer's and library steps. Among their millions that year one walked into a strange land, the wind whipping at her navy skirt and neat white shirt and bow, a stack of textbooks gripped very firmly under a thin arm. It was a big step for a girl so afraid of fear, one who, only a few years before, had cried her heart out in terror in a nun's arms all night.

Now each morning Laura took a subway to school, returning late in the afternoon. The very ability to travel outside the Institution gave her confidence. Her high school homework took all her time, but she continued with Sister Jean's children, becoming ever more skillful with them. Her school results, however, were minimal. She failed many subjects, just passed others. It was hard for me to make her see that, relative to the way she had been, she was doing much more than anyone could ever expect of her.

No, she saw only her failure to achieve, and it was fortunate she had her work with the children to offset this innate defeatism. It is distressing to watch a child who *must* succeed humped disconsolately over a book she cannot understand, as if great boulders weighed on her shoulders and curved neck. Yet already there were teachers who had grown fond of Laura and were unsparing of their time and effort to help her.

Meanwhile, needless to say, all at the Institution did their best to reassure her during those days when the fears of failure gripped her to the point of self-exasperation, and she complained of headaches or colds that made her "too sick" to go to school. The old motto I had seen in my mind over the Institution doors that first day—*Lasciate ogni speranza, voi ch'entrate*—was almost literally reversed. The tears and listlessness with which she met her schoolwork frustrations were sympathetically understood by the nuns. All of us, indeed, were getting used to Laura's ups and downs.

It was in the realm of abstract understanding that she experienced most difficulty. In courses where memorization was required, she did fairly well. However, in the sciences, where she was called on to understand certain principles that were not visible, her grasp failed.

Once, in a fit of such frustration, she told me:

"I know that when an object drops it falls. But how can I understand that there's a force, something called gravity, pulling the object down? I can't see it, can I? I can't feel it, or anything. . . ."

I must admit I was never particularly interested in physics myself, but I tried to demonstrate this concept to Laura. Yet the more I tried to help her with it that afternoon, the more confused she became.

Finally she concluded, "I'm just plain stupid. That's all."

This reaction was by no means without its positive aspects. Failure—once accepted with resignation by her spirit—was now rejected as intolerable. She became incensed by hints of weakness or inadequacy in herself, and was almost too ready to throw herself into new challenges. I tried to explain how there were some things beyond the reach of every individual, that each one of us had to accept some limitations, but she was not in the mood to find this consoling, or even possible. She was like a very young child in many ways, easily frustrated by difficult problems, and quick to give up when she encountered failure.

As the weeks wore on in this fashion, I began to suspect

that this might be a strategic moment at which to approach Laura about a second operation, one to straighten her back. Here was a challenge she had, in a sense, already met in the correction of her strabismus, and had met successfully. I put it to her in the same terms, after having had some lengthy conversations with Sister Margaret.

In a way, I was working against time. While an operation of this nature would mean lost school hours, as well as a disruption of the only recently established new routine in her life, Laura had for her own sake to undergo the operation while still in the Institution. She was now sixteen and in two years' time would be outside the Institution's care, probably on her own and almost certainly unable to meet the expenses.

As a result, Sister Margaret began mesmerizing an orthopedic specialist. At first she seemed to have difficulty in persuading this hapless individual to donate his services free, and my calls of inquiry about the progress of the matter were met by cryptic comments, all too obviously covering up her difficulties.

"I had him on the ropes two days ago, Doctor. But he was saved by the bell. I'll get him in the next round. Just be patient, please."

By now I had little doubt that this gentle nun with the beatific smile would succeed. Sister Paulette called her younger colleague the perfect example of an optimist.

"Once, when Sister Margaret was refused a request by the superintendent," she told me, "I was so surprised that I asked her what had happened. 'Oh,' she replied, 'it was raining out, you know, and this always affects her arthritis. Makes her irritable. On the next warm day she'll feel better and I'll ask her again.' And it happened just like that."

Whether it did or not, I could not say, but I do know that, two weeks later, on a brisk November afternoon, Sister Margaret called me to say that the doctor had finally agreed to take care of Laura without payment.

Children accept medical facts. Laura took her second operation like a trooper. By now she knew what it was like to be anesthetized ("You see a lot of people turning somersaults and then you go to sleep"), and how good the television was in a shared hospital room.

The operation itself—involving a graft of tiny pieces of diced bone taken from the hip and inserted between the vertebrae—took three hours, and Sister Margaret and Mrs. Clancy were there to see her when she came out of it. They told me she was cheerful in her uncomfortable chin-to-hip body cast, and they left her sleeping on an orthopedic mattress.

Soon brought back to the Institution, Laura remained in bed for three months, subject to a series of X-rays, which in fact lasted for years. I visited her there in her dormitory and she seemed to have come through the ordeal with flying colors.

Already she was looking forward to taking care of the younger children again and returning to school. During these months Laura was given daily tutoring in her subjects by one of the nuns who taught in a local parochial high school. Meanwhile another Christmas passed; this one she spent in bed.

The New Year came in and at the end of this prescribed period Laura exchanged her cast for a brace, against which her body was tightly bandaged. When I first saw her walking around in this, I realized that she who had always bent forward like an old lady now had a back as straight as a pin. Worthy of a guardsman! Her confidence soared at the way she looked, but she tired easily and needed lots of rest. It was impossible to push her at this time. At the end of another three months she could take off the brace.

However, this meant she could start going out to school again and resume her contact with her favorite teachers, some of whom now invited her to their homes and treated her like one of the family. Laura always looked forward to these visits.

Life

One early spring day I was just getting ready to leave the Institution when my telephone rang. It was the Quarterback, and I at once knew something was wrong by the tone of her voice. She wanted to see me immediately, about something "confidential."

"I'd rather talk to you about it in person, Doctor."

When I walked into the nun's office a minute later she was alone and looked extremely worried. She came out with it at once:

"We've had a phone call from Laura's father," she said, "and he wants to see her."

I went into a deep silence. And then Sister Margaret said it for me.

"You realize, Doctor, he has a perfect legal right to see his child, since she was not surrendered by her parents."

"Not only to see her," I concurred with a groan, "but to take her."

So all our care had come to this. Dr. Crager had discharged Martin Meyer, as he had hinted he would, and there was nothing in the world to stop the man who had tried to burn his child alive from reclaiming that girl now as his daughter.

How had he found out where she was? That question was easy enough to answer. Laura's case was on file with the Department of Welfare. Any father calling up to say that he had been discharged from a hospital and wanted to contact his daughter would be welcomed by this heavily overburdened agency.

"Shall I ask Laura if she wants to see him, Doctor?"

"Let me talk to him first," I said, but I said it with little hope.

My deepest fear was beginning to turn into reality, and all I could do was watch it come true.

Martin Meyer came in to see me. It was some time since we had met, in C Building, Haltzer, of that huge state mental hospital, but apart from a further graying of his hair, a certain humping of his back, he really looked much the same to me. He wore a suit and dashing tie and lost no time in bringing both to my attention.

"Good to see you, Doc. How you like my new suit?"

His nostrils gave a twitchy fidget. I decided to go straight to the point. I was unsure of how much—at this stage—my patience could be counted on to stand Martin Meyer.

"What do you want, Martin?" I asked.

"Well now, Doc, you shouldn't speak that way to me. You supposed to help people, and to be understanding. I'm surprised at you," he said, with a waggish grin. "Really I am. How'm I going to respect you, if you take that attitude?"

"What attitude?"

"Not bein' glad to see me, I mean."

"I am not glad to see you, Martin," I said, breathing heavily. "Come to the point."

His pale eyes darted under the shelf of his craggy forehead. His hands came out, and he looked at them as they moved before his eyes. His hands said: ironworker, derrick operator, truck driver's . . .

"I want to see my daughter, Laura," he said, in an ominously quiet tone. "After all, a good father ought always to be interested in his child. You should know that, Doc."

"How did you discover she was here, Martin?"

"I have friends." His big hands spread expansively . . . powerfully. "Owed me a few favors. You know what it's like, Doc."

As he rambled on I looked at those hands and I thought of Laura. His assumed calm was, as ever, a fragile crust. I thought of Laura and I thought of all the suffering those horny hands had caused her, each moment of anguish, and untold sorrow, that an abused child . . .

"Okay, Martin," I cut in, staring straight at him. "Let's come to what you're here for. And I mean, really here for."

My hostility drew him short. He kept repeating that I

wasn't like the kind, good doctor he had met once in the hospital. I pushed ever harder at him.

"What do you really want here?"

"Okay. So, okay, you're not glad to see me," he replied, panting slightly and with another nervous twitch of those hairy nostrils. "Maybe I should talk to someone else here."

"You're stuck with me," I told him. "You see, I happen to know your life, Martin, yours and Adeline's, as well as Laura's. I think I know what's going on."

He came back in a sudden cringing whine. "Look, Doc, you're making me nervous. I'm a sick man. You don't know what's it like. Them headaches. I mean, I've been taking pills every day, for my nerves, and you're pushing me and pushing me and there ain't nobody push Martin Meyer around." Suddenly he jammed his square face forward and yelled, "Nobody in this whole wide world tells Martin Meyer where to go."

"So what do you plan to do about it, Martin?" I said to him. "Take a swing at me?"

He calmed at once. "Look, Doc . . . I don't want, for to lose my cool . . . I mean, look, I don't want to fight with you. I jus' want to see my daughter . . . and be a father to her. That's all. Keep calm, Doc . . . Yeah. Can tell when you get angry. Guy like you means business. Well then, we understand each other."

"Exactly," I said. "And I'm not going to let you do anything to hurt Laura, Martin. She's been very sick, she's still very weak, and only just now beginning to get a little better."

He bounded back in his seat. "You crazy, Doc? Me? Me hurt my own daughter? Who do you think I am?"

There was silence between us a second. After our heated exchange it seemed very full.

"Do you really want me to tell you, Martin?" I said.

"Okay, okay, you're smart," he replied, grumbling, yet amicable enough at that moment.

"Well, we'll see," I said finally. "I'm going to let Laura be the one to decide if she wants to see you."

"Will you ask her then, Doc?"

"Sister Margaret will give you our decision in a few days. Good-bye, Martin."

With suspicion in his darting, ferrety eyes, Martin Meyer left me, shambling off down the passage along which his daughter had walked so painfully slowly, so often, and his huge hands trembled at his sides.

I was thinking fast. I had to tell Laura about her father. I slammed the books on my desk. Just how much could a child be expected to take? Here we were threatening her once again. The fact that the man was her father was of course bound to draw her to him. But to what end? To what eventual menace to her personality?

We had left it at that. If Laura wanted to see him, he would be "allowed" to come to visit her in the Institution. I put mental quotes around the word "allowed" since, if she refused, there was nothing to prevent his taking his request to the juvenile courts, where, I knew, he could win this right.

I sat and thought for a long time after Martin Meyer left me. I had perhaps bought a momentary respite for Laura. She had only just gathered strength from one long, tiring battle, and now to have to face this—possibly the most momentous crisis in her life, one that would make all the rest look like a picnic. Ordinarily, the discovery of a father—someone with whom she could feel a strong tie—would be a strengthening experience. But, then, Martin Meyer was not a predictable individual.

I had to face up to the problem of how to tell Laura about him. How do you tell someone her father wants to see her, when he hasn't all her life? How do you field all the inevitable questions like "Where has he been?" and "Why hasn't he been to see me before?" Even if I helped her with all the warnings in the world, I could not expect her to turn her back on him. Her long search for identity had so many missing links, and Martin Meyer was one of them.

Previously, in our many conversations, Laura had refrained —with a kind of exquisite tact—from prying too much into the problem of her parents; it was as if they were part of the past and she was happy to leave them there, at least for the time being. Her main drive was significantly to separate herself from her helplessness and dependency. But I saw that, coming at this moment, the presence of her father would awaken dormant hopes and expectations that might produce in their train a sense of overwhelming disappointment. Laura was still an extremely sensitive plant.

The timing was rotten, but Martin Meyer was someone Laura had to come to terms with sooner or later. She had to be told. I decided to ask her to be sent down to me at once. I reached for my telephone and dialed Sister Jean.

When Laura came in she was looking flushed and fulfilled from her work with the children. She sat down opposite me and I think there was something in my face that must have warned her. She had, after all, come to know me by now almost as well as I knew her.

"Laura," I began, deciding to go straight to the point, "I have something very important to say to you. Your father was here."

"My father!" Color drained from her face as she sat back against the chair with an audible clink of her brace. Momentarily she quailed.

"He was here," I went on, "and he wants to see you."

I let the shock register silently awhile; she looked directly at the wall in front of her. Her dry lips moved, but no sound came. Gradually I told her all I knew about him—insofar as he had been mentally ill and now was living in the community again.

At last, after another lengthy silence, Laura said, "Why does he want to see me?"

I reiterated the reasons Martin Meyer had given, but as

if she hadn't heard a word she repeated the exact same question.

Why, indeed? I made clear her choice in the matter and the fact that I would abide by her decision. I also added some considerable caution as to not expecting too much from him.

Suddenly, her eyes unflinching, her face still white and set, Laura turned to me. "I don't know why, but I must see him. I must talk to him."

The emotion was compelling. She had to come to terms with Martin Meyer. There was no frame of reference, no personal bond with him to recall, he was a man from another planet. But I respected the intensity of her inner need to surmount this obstacle, too.

Later, I walked back alone down the darkened streets to my subway station. The sidewalks were wet with rain. The chill that came at dusk hunched the passers under thin coats or old leather jackets. Army surplus stores did a thriving trade in this neighborhood. Some shivering youth asked me for a dime. Overhead, the stars were out, and I remembered once having told Laura, in one of those endless early monologues when I had been searching for something to say, that the stars were girls going to bed with their candles. Was the wind now snuffing one of these out?

We had not asked for much for Laura—only that life should not be all ugliness. It would be cruel indeed if we had brought her all this way, helped her to become firmer, and indeed more shapely, only to have her wrenched back from us into the morass of brutality and mindless violence from which she had first emerged. How tragic it would be if all her own courage, all the risks she had taken, were to come to nothing after all. Due to Martin Meyer's personal reaction to me, I decided not to be present at the interview between Laura and her father.

Instead, Sister Margaret was there when they met. I was told that Laura smiled when she entered the room, and sat down shyly across from the man who had all but killed her in infancy. The conversation was strained and spasmodic. This was understandable enough. Evidently he asked question after question concerning Laura's life in the Institution; she answered in a subdued, hurried manner. They were together the best part of an hour, and before he left Martin Meyer told his daughter he would call her every night, and that he would see her again the following week.

Here it should be mentioned that to have parents—of whatever kind—gave a girl in the Institution a high degree of status in her group. Such girls were normal, loved, and, by implication, pretty. Somebody cared for them because they had something to offer—if not beauty, then intelligence, ambition, some lovable trait.

In the week that ensued Laura took full advantage of her new-won prestige. She told any listening ear all about her father, how handsome he was, what he did, and how he was coming to see her every week from now on, finally how she would eventually live with him.

All the girls in her group were happy for Laura. Now she would get clothes, money, every Sunday she would eat in a restaurant or go to a movie. Well, perhaps not the movies *every* Sunday. There were so many other places they could visit in the city. With each telling of her meeting, Laura's descriptions became more detailed and fanciful, particularly with regard to the supposed future with her father.

Sister Margaret and I heard these stories with gloom. Was Laura building up for a truly destructive letdown? There seemed no pedestal high enough for her new-found parent, no cloud large enough to contain her expanded sense of importance. It was an all-or-nothing aspiration, with only—so far as I could see—a thundering, one-stop fall to the very bottom as its conclusion.

Each night now she waited patiently near the phone in the corridor outside her room. But no call came. The following week the girls in her room fixed her hair, loaned her their treasured jewelry, and one of them her best dress—the finest in the dormitory, by universal consensus. In fact, there was a shared anxiety of excitement in all the girls, as there was in Laura herself, when the hour of the visit approached. It was a vivid consciousness, half elation, half fear, as the clock chimed the hour. In the mutual tension the striking of the quarter after, and then the half hour, seemed to come in quick succession. The hour passed, and the next, with the strong slow strokes of the Institution clock, until the truth gleamed through to the little gathering of girls, with their wide-open eyes and clenched hands. Her father was not coming. The fatal reverberations of the striking clock ended for Laura in a tempest of hot tears, which left her weary and aching, stretched out on her bed in all her useless finery. Sister Paulette comforted her all night.

Nor did Martin Meyer come the following week. Nor the week after that. The children were the first to make excuses for him. "He was probably tied up at work." Or: "Maybe he got ill, and couldn't come." They did their best to cushion the impact, but Laura turned from them in an unexpected manner.

Frankly, I had been afraid she would crawl back into her shell once more, sitting hopelessly on the side of her bed as she had in the past. Far from it. She became angry, outspoken, critical of everyone and everything. She even began complaining bitterly about the Institution. Then, to the absolute amazement of both the nuns and the school authorities outside, Laura began truanting from school.

At first Sister Margaret simply doubted these reports. There had to be some explanation. The teachers must have made some clerical error, and not noticed Laura sitting in the back of class. Unfortunately, the explanation would not hold water. Laura was carefully checked. She was seen off to school, and she never arrived.

When girls truant it seems to create more concern than when boys do the same thing. I suppose we expect something of this behavior from boys, and are more alarmed at the idea of defenseless girls wandering about a big city alone, which is what such truancy usually involves. But when a girl like Laura was the case in point, the matter was distinctly serious.

In the Institution truancy had to be reported, mandatorily, to the superintendent; and I was given to understand, from Sister Margaret, that the superintendent also questioned whether there might have been some clerical error. But no. Laura truanted for eight days in succession. Where she had been, what subways she had ridden with her few pennies, or parks she had walked through, or perhaps cold beaches she had discovered on the city's rim, no one ever knew. What we did soon learn was that directly she came back she almost immediately got into a fist fight with another girl, a former friend, after a long barrage of name-calling and insults.

It was a new Laura who came back to us. She lashed out at everyone, including the nuns. She seemed full of hate, and was quick to let you know if you got in her way!

I myself saw Laura's anger as an unfortunate but necessary defense against the rejection and hate of those she dared trust. She derived strength from her anger, as it helped diminish her sensitivity and even held her together in a reality that never ceased to remind her that she was unwanted. Her father's betrayal had been a puncturing of her vanity, and this was how she took it out on the world in general. The nuns, however, were understandably uncertain of how to deal with the "new" Laura and repeatedly discussed their amazement over this or that incident. The culmination of this period came when Laura announced that she was fed up with everything, including the superintendent.

"I've been wanting to give her a piece of my mind for a long time," she coolly informed Sister Paulette one afternoon when she had come back from school, "and I think I'll do it now."

Sister Paulette was properly horrified. However, she saw that little good would be served by simply reading out the riot act to Laura and informing her head-on that nobody—

but nobody—gave a piece of her mind to the superintendent, unless perhaps it were the mother superior. She pleaded with Laura in vain for a while. The girl who a little while before could barely hobble down a passage left the room in quick decision, and was last seen heading straight for the superintendent's office.

Frantically, Sister Paulette assembled a caucus of nuns nearby. All agreed that it would be nothing short of a disaster if Laura ever carried out her threat. Operation Kidnap went into action.

This was a complicated and extremely well-co-ordinated maneuver, which perhaps could have been effected only within the walls of something like the Institution. The intention of the exercise was simple: keep Laura busy, and as far away from the superintendent as physically possible, until she "cooled off." The intercommunication was excellent. I personally verified the complete success of Operation Kidnap.

To be sure, there was for a moment a certain hectic buzzing-around of the upstairs nuns and frequent calls to their reserves in other quarters. The first safari to deroute Laura was headed by Sister Jean, who struck off boldly, at full speed, for the superintendent's office. This she approached nonchalantly enough, though with a pang of apprehension at sight of Laura firmly encamped on the long bench outside it. The nun herself, supposed to be calling on her superior in some minor errand, stopped with admirably simulated surprise at sight of her assistant:

"Laura! You're just the person I want to see. I need some urgent help with two of the children."

It was just in time. Laura, waiting for the superintendent to get off the phone, was literally swooped off the bench and kept busy for the rest of that day.

Further strategy had to be devised hastily on the following morning, however, when Laura again announced her intention of "telling the superintendent off." Here the problem was complicated by the fact that Laura was still occasionally truanting, and thus might show up to carry out her threat at any moment of the day. None of the nuns had time to sit and watch for her to appear, nor could they contrive to keep her busy every minute of the day.

The situation looked hopeless until Sister Margaret (of course!) suggested an ingenious plan. Why not bring the superintendent's secretary into their confidence? Then every time Laura showed up outside the office she could send off an emergency call to one or other of the first team. It was agreed that, if the whole of the first team were out, Sister Martha in the kitchen could almost certainly come through with some "urgent" errand. A list of further reserves was drawn up.

Problem. Could the secretary be trusted? It was agreed that this was the one fly in the ointment, and it remained so until Sister Margaret sweetly disclosed that the secretary was related to the husband of one of the reserve team's sisters. This, we were assured, made her part of the family and, indeed, after a few more phone calls, she was easily drafted into service.

Day after day for over a week Operation Kidnap continued its successful career. No staff officer, or perhaps espionage chief, could have felt prouder of his men. Every nun involved made it a point to go out of her way to pass the long bench outside the superintendent's office as she went about her business.

The alarm was sounded by the secretary on half a dozen occasions and, while she stalled for time, a nun would duly appear, trying not to show that she was panting for breath and acting as surprised as possible at coming across Laura, needless to say "just the person I want to see." There was a plea for instant assistance that kept Laura moving from one end of the Institution to the other and, one day, right across town in company with a nun.

I myself got details of the escapade from sisters Margaret and Paulette. They were confused at my laughter. For them it was, it seemed, a fairly routine rescue operation, but I shall not easily forget the sight of the nuns with their robed heads together, whispering here and there as they planned some new scheme to keep Laura busy.

22

When the girls returned from summer camp that year, I again set up a series of appointments with Laura through Mrs. Clancy. To my surprise I now started experiencing some difficulty in seeing her. For the first time in our long relationship Laura refused to come to see me. She broke her appointments. I had evidently now been included—along with the superintendent—among her "bad guys," those she hated.

This was not of great importance, but Laura's increasing disregard for all the rules of the Institution, and the school outside, was. Sullen outbursts were succeeded by periods of tense withdrawal and isolation. Once more she would remain closeted in her room for hour after hour.

It was nearly November when finally I reached Laura. Her young lips quivered as she unleashed her hatred in all directions. Again, she kept mentioning the superintendent and how she was going, one day, to tell her off and then walk out of the Institution forever and live by herself. She did not at that meeting refer to the father who had never again telephoned or come back; after that one visit Martin Meyer had for some reason—who knew? perhaps he was frightened of his own impulses—stayed away from his daughter. But he had left her once more emotionally disturbed. And this was very serious.

Early that November a full staff conference was called in which Laura's case was evaluated. Everyone connected with it in the Institution was present. The theme was simple: was she finally unrecoverable?

For the prosecution, as it were, Dr. Clemente reiterated his initial opinions. He summed up flatly:

"Look, Laura will have to go to a hospital. She is mentally ill and now her behavior gives evidence of deterioration, and in the best interests of all . . ."

I glanced around. One nun, standing in as a sort of deputy for the superintendent, was plainly being convinced of these arguments. After all, the Institution was a large family, the only one most of its children had ever known, and the sisters the only adults who gave the children their reason for living. Laura could not be allowed to disrupt the progress of the majority. Dr. Clemente was his most clinically logical self that day.

Needless to say, Mrs. Clancy at once pitched in on what I called "our" side. Her face red, her gestures strong, she made a fine defense attorney, while our Quarterback and Sister Paulette each added her two cents' worth of opinion in favor of keeping Laura.

I was worried. Here was a deep conflict of therapeutic views between myself and Dr. Clemente. His argument was that she had a "mental illness" and therefore needed "treatment" in a hospital. Books (some of which have been written) are needed to refute these views controllably, but I had only a few minutes at my disposal.

I argued that the word "mental" assumed a circumscribed place in Laura's physical makeup, i.e., the brain, a substance that becomes infected, inflamed, or whose tissues may be destroyed by the damage known as *illness*. No one had found anything wrong with the way Laura's brain functioned; on the contrary, her achievement in speech after the long years of silence was extraordinary. No, her brain did not require some special medical treatment. She was an unhappy, hurt child, little different from the thousands of other children *and adults* (I emphasized) who succumb in their struggles to

204

adapt to their environment. Human beings, rather than any virus or microorganism, were responsible for Laura's failure to adjust. Therefore, it was in the *best* interests of all if she remained; the children in the Institution could help in restoring her faith in herself, and in others.

What's more, I went on, I had not heard of any of the children complaining about Laura. Most of them seemed to be trying to help her. Like so many of us, Laura had succumbed to internal and external stresses, she had hobbled ahead for a while, and now she was faltering. Her faltering was a weakness bred by a long history of maladjustment to an environment that had deprived her of the basic necessities for successful survival. Hospitalization would only exacerbate this condition. The present environment was the only one that held out hope for Laura now.

By laying her case at the doors of society in this way, I am glad to say that we won the decision to retain Laura in the Institution. But it had been an anxious afternoon, one that reminded me of how thin the ice was on which we were all treading here. I willingly accepted the cigarette Mrs. Clancy proffered me back in her cluttered office, as we set up a time for me to get to Laura as soon as possible.

When the day came it needed little prompting to have her tell me what had happened. That she had been deeply disappointed and hurt by her father's "betrayal" was at once apparent in her effort to show how tough and cold and indifferent she was whenever I advanced his name. Meanwhile, the tears that rolled down her cheeks revealed, only too clearly, the anguish in her heart. . . . I decided to play the devil's advocate once again.

"So what did you expect?" I finally asked her, after one particularly intense outburst of disgust. "A nice warm teddy bear that moves his eyes when you want him to and makes you laugh and cuddles you at night?"

Laura cried out, "Oh I knew you were going to say that. I just knew it. That man is *nothing*." She spat out the word with all the venom of which her young being was capable. "Why, he wasn't even man enough to walk out on me without covering up his phoniness by promises he couldn't keep. I hate him, I hate him! I just hope he does call and ask me to see him. I want to give him a taste of his own medicine. He's so low. Spineless. Yes, a spineless creature who brought me into the world and I'm sure glad he never raised me or I would have really flipped my lid."

I calmed her and tried to show her that she would have to look toward people who were capable of giving her love.

"You're right," she answered with a sudden grip on her boiling emotions. "You can't get blood from a stone, I guess. You know, I'm glad I saw him. I had him on this pedestal, oh so high. I pictured him as . . . so great. I used to look at some of the other girls' fathers and say to myself, 'Mine is better.' Now I know that he isn't, and there's no use pretending any more. He just isn't," she concluded with a tremor in her tone, "what I thought."

What was interesting, as we continued our talk, was that Laura had been secretly expecting my remarks. I suspect that, long before I gave her my few words of caution, she sensed that someday she would find out what her father was really like. Now she could resist this truth no longer. The little girl who had held on so tightly to her dreams of one day finding a benevolent, loving father in a world of twinkling teddy bears had now to come to grips with reality. The complicated mixture of infant and adolescent I had dealt with for so long was developing into a mature young lady.

Though now she was prepared to face once more into the future, with that courage so characteristic of her, she admitted how afraid she was of this new emotion, her destructive anger.

"Could I destroy somebody too?" she asked with wondering eyes. "Was this what made me hate the superintendent so? How? Why?"

I tried to explain that she had been punishing herself, in

a token manner. Her feelings of unworthiness—even her refusal to talk—were implicitly by-products of this same internalized emotion, which had lately broken loose, unleashing its violent forces on all those around her, including—in a vicious cycle—herself.

Her refusal to talk had, in fact, all the qualities of a little child getting even with its parents by refusing to open her mouth as they anxiously looked on, holding out a spoon of food. Her retaliation against the world developed into a form of martyrdom in which others were hurt or punished by her own self-destructiveness. The enemy (I repeated) was in herself. Now that she had freed her anger, expressed it in action, she had helped dissipate its strength and bring it under some sort of control; her insidious hunger for revenge would gradually abate.

"I'm sure there are better things to come for you soon, Laura," I said. She reached for my hand and squeezed it tight.

And so there were; Laura calmed, returned regularly to school, and resumed her routine within the Institution walls. In three weeks she was back working for Sister Jean again. I had not seen her recover so rapidly before and took this for an indication of her improvement and growth. In fact, the initial impact of each problem so mobilized her anxieties that her final adaptation was always more integrated than previously. It is often said that it is the highly strung who last longest, emotionally, in battle conditions—they have had to make more and deeper inward demands of themselves in the past. Laura, too, was maturing the hard way. How could any situation be worse than what she had been through already? In her short life she had met, and surmounted, problems that most people don't encounter in a lifetime.

Once the crisis was passed, Laura seemed to become ever more stable and mature, her friendly manner now coinciding with the physical changes that had been slowly taking place since the onset of adolescence. Much of her wan childishness of expression was going now, and the first time I saw her in high heels I could not believe she was only sixteen.

Now it was rare to find her moody or depressed. She had become friendly with two girls in particular and spent a lot of time with them. At the same time, the "cat fights"—as they were locally dubbed—did not always exclude her, either. Sister Jean alone was a little worried about the pain Laura's legs gave her from time to time.

Whenever I caught sight of her in the halls or passages she always waved to me in a friendly manner. All the children seemed to have a warm word to say to Laura as they passed her now. She was keeping up with her group and gaining in confidence and responsibility. The disappointment over her father had taught her life's hard lesson, that all of us must modify our goals at some time. She was observant and lively and we decided that the time had come for her third operation—not the gravest, but by no means the least important psychologically—plastic surgery on her face.

23

The operation was scheduled for the early part of spring. Once again Sister Margaret was able, mysteriously, to cajole or coerce a plastic surgeon into performing it free.

Laura seemed to have mixed feelings about the event. At first I was surprised by this. The burn scars did detract from her appearance, and, after all, she had always made such a point about her ugliness in the past. When I reminded her gently of this, she answered:

"Yes, that was in those days. But I've become used to my face." She gave a quick laugh. "It's the only one I've got."

"It would make you look prettier," I said. "Don't you want that?"

"Oh, you mustn't misunderstand me," she went on at once. "Sure, I want to look attractive, but I also can't help feeling that it doesn't matter all that much. What I want to do is work with young children. That's more important to me than anything in the whole wide world. Oh, I wish you could give me more brains so I could be a nurse!"

In one way this marked a positive change in her values—to have her confidence resting, now, on her usefulness as a person. Yet in another sense it could be one more safety valve, an escape from complete maturity.

Most of the other girls Laura's age in the Institution were interested in boys, often involving themselves in endless emotional problems worthy of some medieval schoolman. Laura had never shown this interest. The other girls spent their pocket money, and much of their time, improving their looks, as she did not.

For Laura's life experience was, of course, far beyond her age, and we did not want her never to know what it was to be young. She was now a serious girl, intent on her work with the children, and apparently resolved never to waste her time on play, extracurricular activities at school, or long telephone conversations with "mere" boys. She preferred classical music to the current rock-'n'-roll. She was almost too devoted to her goals.

So I left the decision about the operation to Laura herself. And one day, when discussing her case with Sister Paulette, the pale nun's serene and serious eyes studied me from under the pleated skin of her forehead as she said:

"I know Laura doesn't fuss like the other girls over her appearance, but maybe if she thought she was as pretty as some of them, she wouldn't mind competing with them on their level. Maybe she's afraid that, even if she has the operation done, boys might not be interested in her."

These were interesting speculations, but I felt that Laura was once more trying to steer away from any deeper involvements in her crowded life for fear of being hurt. Or was she by her hesitation trying to tell me something that I'd missed? Was there danger that another crisis might be provoked at this time? I couldn't answer any of these questions. I had to wait for Laura to give me the answers.

In a sense she began to do so by accepting the facial operation, which, in truth, might well have deterred a mature and stable adult. Up to a certain age children will accept medical facts; if you tell them too much, they stare. If you don't tell them enough, they ask questions. But Laura went into this new operation, masterminded by our Quarterback, with an unusual maturity of understanding; it was, accordingly, an important step in her mental, as well as physical, progress.

Life

The worst of Laura's burns were on the left side of her face, starting at the chin and going up to the eye. Luckily for her, the grafting "took." It does not always do so. There was a little difficulty, and apprehension, caused by the instruction that she might not smile during this period of recovery, but she had been solemn so long in the past that she managed it again now, and, after periodical examinations for any signs of infection and for cleansing, it was simply a matter of changing the dressings and watching the healing process. While in the hospital she became a great favorite with the nurses, and after only two weeks was sent back to the Institution. The surgery had been entirely successful and all she had to do now was to visit her surgeon from time to time to check on progress.

When all the dressings had been removed, Laura seemed content with—but not ecstatic over—her smooth, unmarked white skin. When I visited with her she did not seem in any way anxious or disturbed. The other girls, however, hovered around her incessantly, sighing with amazement, calling in their friends to look at "Laura's new face" and filling her ears with their compliments.

When Laura came to me for her next talk after this, I was still waiting for all the answers to come in. But she merely repeated what she had said before the operation—that she liked the idea of being pretty, yet there were more important things in life. I began to see that I had been a victim of my own doubts and anxieties developed in the course of our long and close relationship.

For Laura's facial scars were the direct result of her being burned in a frying pan when an infant. I knew this; she didn't. All Laura knew was some ego-acceptable story that had been given her long ago, about being the victim of a fire in infancy. So for me the removal of the scars had a symbolic side: now the surgeon's knife had removed forever any reminder of the infamous crime. I must have been expecting her to share something of this significance, forgetting that for her the operation was a simple matter of improving her appearance—important, but not all-important. No, this was one tragedy she never knew about. It was I who had to forget.

I was sitting thinking all this over in my office a week later, when it happened.

I had just seen Laura again. The first approach of summer always introduced a note of uplift into the Institution. One noticed birds in the inner garden, and children gripping the swings there with young, tense fists. Laura herself had seemed much more alive that afternoon, a sense of individuality one noticed in the way she held her hands as much as in her momentary, easy smile. With school coming to an end she was busy preparing herself for her first job outside the Institution. Mrs. Clancy had found her a position with a family on Long Island; Laura would stay with them for the summer and look after their children. It was an exciting prospect for her and we chatted about various details long beyond the hour.

Sitting alone after she had left me, I was idly contemplating my own summer ahead, with some hopes about vacation and a lessening of my winter pace, full of so many steady pressures and tensions—when the telephone shrilled beside me. I picked up the receiver.

Sister Margaret's voice said, "Laura's mother is here in my office."

I recall that I paused so long she had to ask twice over, "Are you there, Doctor?"

Then my insistence that she repeat what she had said did not change what I had feared. I had heard quite correctly the first time; and I knew it.

"She wants to see her daughter," said Sister Margaret solemnly.

I tried to stifle a sigh. I felt tired, drained out. Hadn't

I just been through all this with her husband? Here we went again. I postponed any further discussion about the matter with Sister Margaret and arranged to see the woman on my next visit to the Institution.

24

Frankly, I was curious. What did one say to a woman who had borne a child and then helped torture it as an infant—who had, in fact, been part of a dreadful conspiracy to kill her offspring?

Did one ask if it had started to sprinkle outside yet? Was the weather man wrong once more? And how were the squirrels in Central Park?

What, in turn, did she say? Would she look at the daughter whose life she had all but extinguished and ask, "How've you been, honey?"

I met Laura's mother before she arrived in my office, since the heavy burden of her perfume preceded her like the sound of trumpets announcing a queen. For a second she stood in the doorway, smiling uncertainly, interrogatively, yet in a self-assured manner reminiscent of some fading burlesque queen looking for a job.

Her hair was unevenly bleached. Her rouged cheeks were layered in powder that caked like confectioners' sugar at the lines and wrinkles in the face, which had aged immeasurably since last I'd seen it. Her red and swollen eyes told of lack of sleep. Laughter lines had become crow's-feet. Over fifty now, Adeline was still trying to look under thirty.

With a polite nod and coquettish smile, she minced in, shook my hand, sat down, and began to rattle off an obviously prepared *spiel* about how much she had longed to see her daughter, her beloved girl, Laura.

Pink beads and bandy eyes. I watched the swivelings of her expression as she talked, self-consciously touching her hair, frowning, or lighting cigarette after cigarette. Her lips were dry and there was a vaguely bewildered expression on her face most of the time, but it was her hands that betrayed her age.

Every now and then she giggled, or lapsed into a rasping cough and a tirade against the polluted air we breathe within the city. A twitch on the left side of her face even caused some of the face powder to fall to her lap, after which she would dust frenetically at her cotton dress. I soon established that she did not know where her husband was, any more than Martin knew where she was at this moment.

"Life's been hard for me, Doctor," said Adeline Meyer, frowning as she tapped off her ash. "All that trouble with my husband, I mean. Like it never seems to end. A cruel man, Doctor, you don't know what I suffered because of him."

I murmured something consoling.

"Yeah, all those nervous breakdowns I had because of him. For the past fifteen, sixteen years you could say I been in and out of . . ."

Her memory failed, bothering her as she sought for dates and places. She rubbed her head at this exhausting effort and more powder tumbled to her lap, to be energetically brushed off again. Mrs. Meyer wanted to show me she was a self-respecting woman, and no mistake.

"Yeah, I was sick. Mental, you might say. Oh, my husband was impossible. Of course, I worked when I could. Though the jobs didn't last. Well, I drank, but not any more. No, sir. I'm on the wagon. Even gone to A.A. meetings, y'know it? Right. Everything is now under—firm—control."

"Are you working at the present time, Mrs. Meyer?"

I asked tentatively, only to regret the question directly it was uttered. She gave me a hostile stare.

"I could pick up any number of jobs, Doctor. Just don't care to. Haven't decided which one I will have. Mind you, I done factory, typist, cleaning woman, you name it. But no, I don't drink any more. Didn't I just tell you that? I forget things. Never did have a good memory, y'know." She sat back behind a wreath of smoke and shot me a calculating look. "What I come for is to see Laura. That's my daughter."

"She's fine," I said.

"Must be a big girl now. Bet she looks just like her mother," she tried, stubbing out her barely smoked butt with a winsome smile. "What a beautiful child. Does she ever ask for me? Oh I thought so much about her. Yes, there were many times when I wished to see my Laura."

"Why didn't you come before, Mrs. Meyer?" I asked. She gestured weakly. "There were reasons."

She rambled on, talking compulsively, and leaving me, for the most part, way behind, trying to follow an endless, uncharted stream of consciousness, attached first to one thing, then another.

"See, I have these pictures of Laura when she was just an infant . . . now don't misunderstand me, Doc. I always loved my child."

"Always?"

"Well, there were times when I was too sick to care for her. You probably even feel sorry for me. Well, *don't!*" she snapped suddenly. "I don't need your pity." Her mouth went hard. "All I want from you is my baby. She's mine. D'you hear, Doctor? You can't keep her from me. I'm her mother, ain't I? I can prove it. The law . . ."

"Do you understand?" I began, only to find her interrupting me harshly.

"Understand nothing! I'm her mother. Laura's mother. Why d'you ask me all these questions?"

"I haven't asked you a lot of questions."

"Yeah, you're smart. That neat suit. *I* know. You let me talk so's you can say I'm crazy. Well, I'm not. Ask the doctors at the hospital. They'll tell you I'm cured. There's nothing wrong with me. And I want my daughter back."

"Do you have a job at the moment?" I inserted in the silence that ensued.

"Not exactly. But there's one waiting for me," she hastened to assure me. "There's the future ahead. See. I can help Laura. Give her things. Maybe even make a home for her."

I looked at this woman as she lit another cigarette with almost frantic fingers. Who was I to judge? The record I had read on her in the hospital that distant day flamed in front of me: raped by her brother at the age of ten, beaten incessantly by a sadistic father, thrown out of her home at eighteen, and at twenty-two arrested on a charge of prostitution. . . . It was written not only in the record, not only on the face in front of me, but on the heart of society around us both.

"Do you have a home, Adeline?" I asked her gently then.

"Well"—still indignantly—"you could say that I live in, like, a furnished room right now. That's until I settle my affairs."

"Meaning?"

"You doctors. You think you know all the goddamn answers. To you everyone is just a case. And all the cases fit into some file. Right? Why are you trying to confuse me by putting words into my mouth? All right, I'm smart too. I never went to school or nothing, like you. But I learned a thing or two, I don't mind telling you. Just you remember this—everything we say in here is strictly *confidential*. Like a priest, you can't testify against me."

She beat out the words with a hamlike hand on my desk.

"What have you done recently?" I asked.

"I didn't say I did nothing. Gee, you keep twisting what I mean."

"I'm sorry."

"I'll bet you're sorry, mister," she burst out. "Like shit you're sorry. What you got to be sorry about? Sitting behin' that desk like, like some judge. You're sorry. That's rich. Really it is. When was the last time you scrubbed a filthy factory bathroom, I'd like to ask? And you know something?"

"What?"

"Okay, smarty, so listen. I was born in the slums, raised in the slums, and I lived my goddamn life in the slums. Consistent, huh? Well, I was. You ever do anything about the slums, Doctor?"

I paused. "Why are you angry at me, Adeline?"

"I'm angry at everybody. Your hands ain't clean. If I had your breaks . . ."

"You want me to feel sorry for you, is that it?"

"I just came here to see the kid. You upset me, Doctor. They told me in the hospital, like, I shouldn't get upset. The thing has been my husband. Also, I have this bad liver. They told me, see. It comes from aggravation and, boy, I've had my share of it. You realize I almost lost Laura at birth. Only a mother knows the suffering that . . ."

"Laura's safe and well," I assured her.

"Gee. I wanted to write her. But then I was sick. Well, I didn't know what to say. Didn't even know where she was. I love that child."

"What do you love about her, Adeline?"

For the first time since she'd entered the room she was silent for a long time.

"You ask funny questions," she said at last, wagging her head like some terrier shaking a rat and cascading the flour of her powder on her lap. "I don't know how to figure you out, Doctor. All I want is, can I see my daughter?"

I stalled. "Do you mean, will I point her out to you so you can see what she looks like?"

"I want to talk to her, Doctor."

"About what?"

"What? Well, I don't know. I mean . . . now you're confusing me again. At least I can visit her and she can visit me."

"You can be friends," I prompted.

"Right."

I paused again. "Why should Laura see you?"

"Because I'm her mother," came the indignant reply, "and I love her."

"Would you be very disappointed if it didn't turn out just as you had planned it?"

"Why shouldn't it?" she asked suspiciously, shifting to the edge of her chair.

I saw that this had to be the end of our interview. The woman's conscience was like Swiss cheese. Moral obliquity confers a kind of strength. The powder that flaked off her face was like the past she shucked off at will. A vain woman, aware of her declining powers to attract, she was playing a game with no holds barred. She had a daughter, and now she wanted her. I knew the city departments well enough to recognize that they would put up no block. It was all so gloriously simple. Love was a Mother's Day card. She and Laura would let bygones be bygones . . . indeed, I could visualize her using precisely those worn-out clichés on my patient.

Laura was real. This was Adeline's chance to hold back the advancing clouds of her loneliness, the dark shadows of old age. I saw that this second claim on Laura's future was, in its way, even more compelling. It was going to be harder to shake off Adeline than Martin Meyer. In fact, only Laura could do it. Her future was in her own hands now.

I said, "I'll tell Laura that her mother wants to see her. We'll make an appointment for you in a week. How's that?"

25

Laura paused as she came into my office the afternoon before she was due to see Adeline Meyer. As I looked up and greeted this self-possessed and good-looking girl I realized that by now she could pick up every smallest nuance in my behavior. She knew I had something to tell her.

Sure enough, she came forward, smiled, sat down and spoke before I did:

"Every time you have something on your mind, your face tells me before you do. Why don't you light a cigarette like you always do? . . . There. That's much better. Now tell me what it is you find so difficult to say."

I smiled, too, at this reversal of our roles. "It is hard, I admit, Laura," I confessed.

"I can take it," she replied at once. "Come on. Did I flunk that test in school? Oh, I know. I don't have a summer job, after all."

"No. It's your mother. She wants to see you."

"My *what!*" She sat back, stunned. "Did you say my mother?"

I nodded. "She wants to see you, Laura."

Her troubled eyes strayed as she pushed a strand of fair hair off her forehead. "My mother was buried . . . we had that wonderful funeral . . . we cooked together . . . you remember . . . she danced, she brought me shoes . . . oh, she looked so peaceful when she died." Then Laura stared me in the eyes. "What does she want?"

"To see you, it seems."

"Why hasn't she come before? Or has she?"

I shook my head. "She's been in and out of hospitals and says she had difficulty in locating you."

"Is that what she told you? What a liar!" She bowed her head and was silent for a few moments.

When she looked up there was a trace of a tear in one eye. "I suppose I should see her. In fact, I must see her, mustn't I? I'll see her and I'll be respectful and, and . . . I think I feel sick. Am I getting very confused? When do I see her?"

"Tomorrow. If you want to."

"Yes, perhaps if I do, then she'll go away and never come back and it'll be like she died and I'll be able to remember my mother's face when I saw it last, in the coffin. I don't believe a thing she says. She's a liar, do you hear me?" Laura struck her forehead with her fists. "A liar, a liar! I don't believe she's been away all these years and couldn't find me. This woman's not my mother."

Then the tears came. She crumpled in the chair, forlorn, clutching herself as if helplessly weighted, refuting her grief. I let her stay so for a moment, hearing the patter of women's feet outside, and then light laughter. There had been a little dormitory playlet Laura had helped her charges stage in pantomine last Christmas, about Ruth, and Naomi, and all the sorrow in the world. . . .

"No," I said at last. "She's not dead, Laura. She's alive."

She lifted her tear-streaked face, on which, it seemed, her flayed soul lay exposed. "What does she look like?" she asked. "Is she very pretty? I always pictured her with this beautiful hair, soft skin. Is she old, maybe?"

"About fifty."

"That *is* old. Gee, women get old quickly, don't they. Is she well now?"

I paused, then I nodded. "Yes."

Very quietly, almost numbly, Laura said, "What does she come here for? I don't want any more pain. I'm so afraid. I can't love her." She chewed on a knuckle for an instant. "I loved her, wanted her, worshiped her. But I'm frightened and I hate her. Don't you see, I have nothing to give. I don't want to feel bad again. Please. Please no more pain," she said fervently, "please. I don't know her. You have to love someone, then you trust them." Laura looked at me imploringly. "Isn't that right? You have to love someone . . . don't you?"

I could see the intense push and pull of her emotions. I did not know how to help her.

"Sister Margaret will be there with you, Laura."

"Like last time?" she asked me bravely.

"Like last time," I said, touching her hand.

And it was our ever-compassionate Quarterback who gave me an account of that strange meeting:

"Frankly, they knew they were mother and daughter only because I introduced them. They dragged through a lot of small talk like strangers on a bus. Laura parried anything personal with the finesse of a fencer. You'd have been proud of her, Doctor. Courteous, but distant. Finally, her mother became more and more exasperated at the lack of warmth in her long-lost daughter, and the sugar coating of her comments grew pretty thin. She started snapping at Laura about her hair, how her clothes needed a press, though of course —this was a sidelong glance at me—this 'dump' was only an institution and was obviously neglecting her, et cetera, et cetera. At which point, she said, 'Look what I've brought you, Laura.' The woman reached down for a large paper shopping bag at her feet and pushed it over. 'Go on, see inside,' she encouraged. Laura had been getting more and more uncomfortable under the harshening tirade and shot me a questioning look. I'm afraid I nodded, and so she reached into the bag and pulled out five or six pairs of old shoes tied together. For some reason the effect was electric. Perhaps you know why, Doctor. I don't. For Laura stared at them as though they were snakes, and then, like an exploding volcano, she flung them on the floor and backed away to the nearest wall, crying and yelling, 'You're not my mother, you're a liar, I don't need your old shoes. Go away! Go away!' And then she ran into my arms."

"What happened after that?" I asked.

"Well, her mother couldn't understand the outburst any more than I could. After all, they were only ordinary shoes. Old. But just shoes. You know that our children wear out a lot of pairs of shoes, Doctor, and actually a gift of shoes, even second-hand ones like these, is often brought. So I didn't really understand why Laura was so upset. However, I comforted her as best I might while her mother went on about how ungrateful she was, and spoiled, and undeserving. Finally, I lost patience with this woman and started to give her a piece of my mind. I asked her to leave, and she did."

Once again Sister Margaret must have wondered why it was that I was smiling. I explained how for Laura this had been an extraordinary coincidence. For the beloved mother of her fantasies had had as an essential property the fact that she always brought Laura new shoes; so when Adeline Meyer produced the bag of used and scuffed shoes she played right into Laura's hands. She *could* not be her mother after that!

The nun shook her head, smiling wonderingly. "Anyway, Doctor, she promised to call. Perhaps I should say, she has threatened to call."

But, in the weeks that followed, no call came. In any event Laura had sworn to refuse to speak to her, or see her, again. Adeline faded from her life as had Martin.

As Laura herself explained it to me:

"She wasn't real. Her face was like a mask. Ugh! There

was no one behind it. Believe me, I tried. I kept saying to myself, 'This is your mother and you must respect her.' But yet there was nothing soft, or warm, that I could touch. I had this strange feeling all the time that none of this was happening. I was imagining it all. Nothing happened *inside of me*. You understand, don't you?"

I assured her I did.

"I couldn't find her heart. And that scared me. Then suddenly, like some horrible nightmare, she produced these awful old shoes and that's when I lost control of myself. I mean, I felt I was going out of my mind. The mother I truly loved always brought me new shoes, and so something happened to me deep down. This woman was a liar. I couldn't be two people, could I? I couldn't be what she wanted. It was like talking a different language. My real mother is someone I shall never know or understand. But I'm glad we met. I really don't have a reason for seeing her again."

Such was Laura's last great moment of truth. She had achieved a personal victory unequaled in all her past life. It was not a matter of hating her mother, of revenge, born of disappointment. It was a question of her own identity, of her integrity and wholeness, her honesty to herself—her humanity in the fullest sense. To play the role of dutiful daughter, while feeling nothing for the part, would have been a treachery to her growing inner consciousness.

So the vicious cycle had been broken at last, and by her own efforts. By judging her mother, Laura was beginning to find herself. She was human. That inner strength, which could help her to see Adeline Meyer as a superficial, empty, and even rather sad individual, was the fruit of the human love Laura had experienced, here, inside these stone walls. An ironic twist, indeed, that in this case the force of separation between mother and daughter was love, not hate.

I likened Laura in my mind to one of those graceful

palm trees that bend with the wind, but return upright when the storm is over. Now the summer was at hand and she was looking forward to her first job outside the Institution.

26

More than one girl was hired as summer "mother's helper" from the Institution. The hiring families were usually well-off and living high off the hog in so-called exurbia, in mort-gaged homes densely forested with gadgetry of the type that requires a permanent maintenance crew.

Mr. and Mrs. Ross proved no exception. Their vacation consisted in turning over the care of their three children to an adolescent girl from the Institution. The girls themselves knew they were so much sweatshop labor. However, there was little choice open to them and most yearned for a breath of the country air that the assignment provided. The Rosses had two cars and a ranch-type house with swimming pool on Long Island. All of this impressed Laura at first. Later she was to tell me that the smell of wet, cut grass was a living poem to her.

The children were two, three, and five years of age, all girls. Laura fed the youngest, played with the older ones or read them stories. By now she was expert at capturing the imagination of little children in this way, by dramatic por-trayals of each character in the book; and soon the three were eating out of her hand.

Unfortunately she found herself with less and less time to spend with them. Every morning a long list was hung up by Mrs. Ross of "little things to get done," not ex-cluding what appeared to be the household's winter ironing, saved up on purpose. At first Laura submitted docilely enough to the accumulation of chores, but she was suffering now from more and more weariness in her legs, owing to her varicose veins. The exploitation evidently continued until one day, after having been bitterly upbraided by Mrs. Ross for some peccadillo, Laura ran away. She had failed again, or so she thought; and success, in this her first job, had meant much to her, imagining how she would be able to tell the other girls of her experiences on return.

As she told of it later, she just took a train and got off at Penn Station, miserable and tearful. Shortly after midnight she bought a cup of coffee in a downtown Nedick's, and about 3 A.M. started to panic and make back for the Institution, whose bell she pressed over and over.

But the place was at this time deserted, except for three elderly nuns who acted as summer caretakers. Finally she was let in and, exhausted, wolfed a bowl of soup in the vast empty kitchen. She slept until eleven next morning in a small room to which she was escorted just off the convent.

Laura begged to be allowed to stay with the three old nuns, rather than be sent out to camp to join the others, which would mean, for her, confrontation with criticism. This she was in fact permitted to do, staying with a parochial schoolteacher and eating in and working around the Institution.

I learned all of this when I returned to my routine of appointments in September. I soon found the smiling, happy girl I had left in June deeply saddened by this small experience, one most of us would shrug off as trivial. It had been, in a sense, her first brush with the outside world. She was more than ever reluctant to face the new school year, with its challenges and competitions. Even her job with Sister Jean seemed in jeopardy.

She talked to me a lot of Mrs. Ross, showing a precocious understanding of the woman's motivations. She ended up one day: "You know what? Children aren't like that. They seem to be the only ones who can be themselves, who don't have to pretend. I trust them for that reason. I guess that's why I love being with them. Can you understand that?" She peered at me as if puzzled for a moment, and when I didn't at once reply, she rattled on, "You're different from most grownups, but you also pretend. You wear a mask. You're a doctor and that's the part you play. Are you"—and she paused—"different as a person?"

"What do you think, Laura?" I said.

"You're kind. That face of yours tells me that. You know, you're the first person I ever trusted."

"I'm glad," I said.

When she left me I found myself wondering about this harsh world of ours Laura would soon have to enter. There was so much struggle for her ahead. To start with, she had to work twice as hard as her classmates, just to keep her head above water. At the same time, she knew that this was the only way she could realize her ambition of being a baby nurse. I was not entirely happy about her putting all her eggs into one basket like this, but I had to acknowledge it as a logical choice.

And as I tried to assist her with her work I couldn't help thinking it strange that we should demand high competence in geography, history, and economics as prerequisites for caring for children. Vividly I recollected the large number of healthy mothers I had known who had never gone beyond the third grade, yet were entirely capable of taking care of their youngsters. The fact, however, remained—without a diploma and high marks, no nursing school would accept Laura. This was the world she had to live in, the world we had to live in, too.

Her seventeenth birthday came. All the children adored birthdays. With so many girls in the Institution there was bound to be a party—replete with birthday cake baked by Sister Martha, presents, innumerable cards—at least three times a week. Ice cream flowed like wine on these occasions, which never failed to brighten the heart of even the unhappiest child, let alone capture the enthusiasm of the nuns in attendance.

It should be mentioned that each of these parties organized by the nuns was the result of long hours, late into many a night, of communal labor. It was customary for a sister to be host to sixty or seventy children or more. That meant baking a tremendous amount of cake, and the senior girls helped Sister Martha.

Laura's party was planned with the care of a De Mille spectacular. Invitations were showered around the Institution, and outside it, too.

I was there for the party. She entered the room in a short organdy dress, cheap perhaps but becoming, and as the crowd of friends and nuns began to sing "Happy birthday to you . . ." her face lit just as I remembered it had when she was younger—spontaneously, preciously. She walked straight to Sister Paulette and gave her a big hug.

The presents Laura received were fascinating. Mostly, the nuns gave her clothes and other necessities, but the children, with their limited funds, had to be highly creative in the gifts they gave. The number of handmade potholders and embroidered towels Laura received that day could have started her in a small business.

"Thank you, Susan," said Laura gently, and again, "Thank you so much. This was *exactly* what I needed."

Then there were the presents given by two or three girls together; they had combined to buy a bottle of toilet water or inexpensive perfume. Others gave hand-painted birthday cards, or paintings they had done especially for her.

"Thank you, thank you, Carmela," she said.

A small, beaded pocketbook, involving hours and hours of patient workmanship, had been thrust upon her. Each gift captured the spirit of the child giving it, as well as her feeling for the particular girl for whom it was intended.

The nuns, in turn, grew more and more involved, oohing and aahing as each present was opened, and in their excitement clustered around Laura, obstructing the view of the little ones—who soon vociferated their disapproval. Either they climbed into some older child's arms or, having unsuccessfully tugged at a nun's habit, crawled on hands and knees under a sister's legs to the front to get a better look.

I stood to one side, near the dressing table on which she had set out all her birthday cards, including the one I had sent her. She caught sight of me and smiled, and in a moment disengaged herself and came over.

"Happy birthday, Laura," I said. She would have one more birthday, in the following November, and then in January she would have to graduate from high school. No girl over eighteen could stay on in the Institution. As I looked into her calm young face I wondered how she would survive— alone. If she faltered, there would be no one to turn to. I had tempted her out of the world of fantasy and now she would soon be thrust into the indifferent vortex of the big city, where loneliness could be acute, and would surely grip her, too, with its fears. "Many happy returns," I said with meaning.

She took my hand and squeezed it firmly. "Thank you so much for the present. It was *just* what I needed."

I had given her a small manicure set.

"You certainly got your share of cards," I observed.

There was one that was larger, more elaborate, more garish than the rest. I bent to examine its message:

A mother's love makes children grow, and as you
Grew I loved you more. I watched you walk,
I watched you talk, and hold my hand, and now . . .

It must have been something close to gallows humor that made Adeline Meyer choose a card like that. And if she didn't read the message, then she was as insensitive as Laura had sized her up to be. I put it down in disgust.

Laura nodded. "You read what it said? . . . You know,

I'm such a fool I sometimes think I make my own unhappiness. When the card came, with her name on the envelope, I was afraid to open it because I didn't want to read words of love to me from her. I waited two whole days before I opened that envelope. Even as I finally did so I started to cry, and the more I tried to restrain myself, the more I had to cry. Silly, wasn't it?"

"I don't think so," I said.

"Then I read the words and suddenly became quite numb. They numbed me clear through. My tears stopped. I felt angry and full of hate. Do you know, she even called me on the phone the other night?"

"I didn't know that."

"Well, it was just what I wanted. I hung up right in her face. What a feeling of pleasure. I'm beginning to understand what a strange feeling hatred gives you. You know something? I really hate hating!" She smiled and went on, "Must be like a cop who has to shoot a criminal threatening to kill him. I don't think the cop can like how he feels, but he has to do it. Is the only way to survive to hate, to take advantage of the other person before he gets you? Like animals in a jungle, kind of?"

"No."

"Oh God!" She bent her head a moment. "Today I feel like the tiniest, the very most insignificant insect in the whole wide world, with everyone looking to eat me!"

"You needn't," I said.

But she had turned and left me. Two demanding children were already tugging at her skirt, begging her to open a particularly enticing-looking present.

Laura had been talking about a lot more than just her hatred for her mother. She was becoming painfully aware of her own powerlessness in the world she would have to join outside, that "jungle" where hatred would at times seem a tempting weapon of protection, yet one that would only drive her further into herself.

No Language But a Cry

As each day now drew Laura closer to leaving the Institution, my doubts increased about her ability to survive in our metropolitan jungle outside its protective walls. But there was little recourse except to doubt my doubts. Frankly, there was not much more we could do for her now. Her life lay ahead. As a new spring awoke the earth once more she developed a fondness for flowers, and on weekends could be seen trimming the hedges of the gardens, watering beds, or helping the nun in charge plant some lawn seed or new lilac bush someone had donated.

The problem of another summer came up. Laura was by now game enough to go to work for another family, if we found her one, but I suggested an alternative plan. For there was perhaps one last thing we could do for Laura.

As an infant she had had a severe case of varicosis. Her legs still swelled, particularly when she had been on her feet for a long time. To take on nursing, then, she needed surgery for her varicose veins. If she did not get this problem solved before leaving us, I felt sure it would be years before she could amass the resources to do so. And at the same time she could not afford to be out of school, since this would put her in danger of failing. The end of the school year was thus the logical time for the operation to be performed, and Sister Margaret, needless to say, the logical person to arrange it. I took a deep breath and planned to meet her "by accident on purpose." To date she had a perfect score in the manipulation of hospital administration, but surely there was a limit to even *her* powers of persuasion.

27

I "chanced on" Sister Margaret in the cafeteria a week later.

"Would you care to have a cup of coffee with me, Sister?" I asked as casually as I could. "Spring's early this year, isn't it?"

While I poured the coffee at the corner table, the nun of the angelic smile looked up. "Give it to me straight, Doctor. You have that look that spells 'I need something for Laura.'"

I gave it to her straight. There was no use prevaricating with this member of the team.

When I had finished she took a generous gulp of coffee, set down her cup with a cheerful clink, pushed back her wide black sleeves and said, "Good heavens, I thought you were going to ask me something hard. I know just the doctor we can ask."

"You do?" I said. Poor fellow, was what I thought.

"Yes, and next week when I go on retreat I will pray that Sister Marion—she is the administrator of that same hospital, you know—will continue to be encouraged by the good Lord to pay little attention to the board of directors of the hospital, and will give us one of their rooms. Oh, I can't tell you how annoyed I get with all these papers, papers, procedures, policies, more papers. Sometimes I think I spend half my life signing silly papers. It's just as well I don't spend the other half reading them, isn't it! What else did you have on your mind, Doctor?"

She was right once more. I did have other things on my
mind—like what would Laura do during the rest of the summer after the operation? Sister suggested we speak with Sister
Paulette and Mrs. Clancy to see what we could arrive at by
way of helping Laura with her ambitions. Mrs. Clancy happened to be grabbing an early lunch at another table and soon
brought her corned beef hash and steaming mug of coffee
over to join us. Sister Paulette had to be called on intercom,
but she quickly responded and we were in caucus.

I didn't hesitate to let these women know how I felt about
the families who were looking for a "mother's helper," or
underpaid slavery. Laura had been through enough with Mrs.
Ross.

Sister Paulette suggested employing her at the camp, where
she could continue to take care of the very young ones.

While there was majority agreement on this excellent idea,
Mrs. Clancy kept reminding us of the law that prohibits children from being paid employees of the Institution.

"She becomes like our paid help," Mrs. Clancy concluded
with a forceful gesture of her cigarette. "And that's against
the law."

Sister Margaret gently demurred. "Maybe there's something
I can do about that. We've been paying Laura by drawing
her salary from the 'miscellaneous' fund. So."

"So?" said Mrs. Clancy, looking bravely baffled.

"Well, I don't see why we can't continue the practice at
camp. After all," said Sister Margaret rather majestically,
"miscellaneous is miscellaneous, no matter how you look at it."

I confessed that I found this accountancy legerdemain para-
doxical, and I saw by the quizzical frowns on the faces of
Mrs. Clancy and Sister Paulette that they didn't quite get the
Talmudic logic of it, either. However, they seemed vaguely
satisfied by the nun's answer, or double-talk. It was decided
to "continue the practice at camp."

I couldn't help reflecting that one of these fine days someone was going to be foolish enough to question Sister Mar-

234

garet about this "miscellaneous" fund from which she was drawing Laura's salary, medical expenses, and heaven knows what else. I was willing to bet that by the end of the year the total spent from this fund would exceed the whole Institution food bill. An accountant's nightmare!

Yet, at the same time, I felt equally certain that Sister Margaret would leave the questioner with the feeling that he had received a perfectly methodological explanation for what she had done—even though he wouldn't understand a word of it! The combination of her immaculate habit, the feminine expression on her face, together with her even, mesmerizing manner, conveyed a sense of complete thoroughness and precision that was entirely disarming. Only very occasionally—to those of us who knew her best—did the smile on her face betray how much she enjoyed her tongue-in-cheek maneuverings.

By this point in our conference my Machiavellian nun was well warmed up, sleeves pushed back beyond the elbows as if ready to tackle any task we could present her. But even Sister Margaret's special brand of magic had its necessary limits. Laura would shortly have to leave the Institution forever.

We discussed this inescapable fact, and Laura's personal ambitions. There was a disquieting anxiety in our voices as each of us tried to mask our concern about her future. What kind of work could she do? Housekeeper, office clerk, factory employee—we tossed every idea possible around, knowing full well in our hearts that Laura would not be happy in any such jobs. We knew she would only be really happy working with children and, as things stood right now, this was impossible to achieve.

It was I who used the word "impossible." Sister Margaret pounced on it at once. She seemed incensed by the adjective. " 'The difficult takes time,' " she quoted heatedly, " 'the impossible we do immediately.' We've faced the impossible here more times than you can imagine, Doctor. We can certainly do so again."

Sister Paulette mentioned at this point that there were private schools that offered full courses in baby nursing, leading to a diploma. The graduates of these schools were employed by hospitals, institutions, and private families that needed someone to care for an infant while the mother was regaining her health. The course took twelve weeks of intensive study.

"There you are," said Sister Margaret grandly, staring at me. "What did I tell you? It's exactly what Laura needs."

Mrs. Clancy, who had finished her lunch and was now chain-smoking, shifted to the edge of her chair. "Private school? What are you talking about, Sister Margaret? The superintendent would never agree, and the board of directors would never agree. They'd laugh at us. We just don't have the funds. We'd never get approval, never."

Sister Margaret had lowered her eyes during this outburst. Without looking up she said, "I find the word 'never' equally terminal, like death, and while we can still breathe I prefer to use expressions such as 'may not' or 'unlikely.'"

There was a respectful, if somewhat stunned, silence around our table, but we did not think our Quarterback had appreciably advanced the solution of the problem. Once more we were mistaken.

"You see, Mrs. Clancy," she went on, in the same subdued tone, "your conclusion is correct only if one accepts your premise."

"By which you mean?" asked Mrs. Clancy quickly.

"That is to say, if we *ask* the superintendent and the board of directors, then their answer will be no. I propose that we avoid the word 'never' simply by not asking either of them. Then," she looked up with a smile, "the outlook, I am sure you will agree, becomes much more positive.

"Naturally we *would* need the superintendent's approval

with any program we decide for Laura," Sister Margaret went on in her calm, even manner. "I think, if you check, you will find that the budget does provide funds for educational assistance to any girl who is in need of such help due to an educational handicap. You will all, of course, agree that Laura needs the money to go to school to overcome just such a handicap, so that she can find employment suitable to her talents. In a broad sense we are simply *tutoring* Laura in an area of study she was unable to grasp fully on her own."

Mrs. Clancy broke the silence that succeeded this sally by asking, rather dully, "Uh . . . *broad* sense?"

"Which particular item in the budget were you actually thinking about?" inquired Sister Paulette, puzzled.

"The Remedial Education Fund," came back Sister Margaret placidly.

"But that's used only for tutoring a child in reading, or arithmetic, or the like."

Mrs. Clancy stood up abruptly. "What on earth does a course in baby nursing have to do with learning to read, or arithmetic?"

"Well, you see, Mrs. Clancy," came back the carefully modulated answer, "it is remedial in the sense that the course will correct a situation that normally would not have existed if Laura could read more rapidly and enter nursing school. It is educational in that she will learn something she didn't know before. Maybe for some other child the term *Remedial Education* does mean help with reading and arithmetic. For Laura it means a course in baby nursing. Now do you understand?"

Mrs. Clancy looked as if she had been hit by a revolving door. Every objection she had made so far had been answered by this nun-semantic. She threw in the sponge.

"Since you're so sure of yourself, Sister Margaret, I suggest you handle the whole situation."

When we left the cafeteria Mrs. Clancy walked out with me. She looked somewhat exhausted.

"Doctor," she asked, "do you ever have trouble understanding Sister Margaret?"

"Of course not," I answered brightly. "Why?"

"Oh, I just wondered. No particular reason."

28

Sister Jean was especially happy that Laura was having her legs attended to; she had more and more frequently asked what it was that was paining her assistant, but Laura denied that anything was wrong. Yet the nun noticed she sat down whenever she had a chance. More lately still, Sister Paulette had caught Laura putting hot towels on her legs, and again, when questioned, denying any particular fatigue.

This was typical of Laura's stoic attitude, and determination to hold on to the job of looking after the young ones, which she feared might be taken from her if she showed herself in any way inadequate. Once again I felt the surgery planned would relieve not only her outer pain but her inner fears as well.

When I talked to her about the problem, in fact, emphasizing how nice her legs would look once the bulging blue veins had been removed and the scars covered over by plastic surgery, she exclaimed:

"Oh, my legs don't bother me."

But we knew that the pain, after any prolonged standing, could actually become unbearable, and that Laura was simply afraid to tell anyone about it.

I saw tears forming in her eyes again, as once more I hastened to reassure her about the operation—that it would make her feel better and that of course she could go back to her children afterward. She buried her head in her hands for a moment. It was far from the first, and not the last time I saw Laura weep. Pain was the emotion she knew best of all and had lived with all her life. Happiness was something rather new. It needed handling. Happiness caused her to cry.

On the day of the operation Mrs. Clancy drove Laura to the hospital and stayed with her until she underwent surgery. All went well and Laura's recovery was normal. In the weeks that followed she regained her strength and was given permission to go back to her work.

Moreover, that summer at camp Laura was observed running, jumping, and playing with the children with a vigor no one had seen her capable of before.

Now in a few months she would be eighteen and graduating from high school shortly after this. I still saw her regularly and soon noticed that the possibility of becoming a baby nurse was bothering her. Some of her teachers were definitely discouraging the notion, since her marks were not high enough for admission to any regular nursing school. For my part, I could not overly encourage her in this wish until I knew how successfully our Quarterback had "operated."

Then one October afternoon I found on my desk a note in Sister Margaret's wide-spread scrawl. It read as follows:

I am happy to tell you that I spoke to the superintendent about Laura attending a private baby-nursing school and she is in full accord with the plan. She was not quite sure this was covered by our budget since the tuition exceeds the amount of money we have. However, the budget does adequately cover about half of the tuition. The other half will be drawn from our "miscellaneous fund," about which I think I have talked to you; this is because we don't have any other category in the budget that adequately covers such items as uniforms, books, etc. The arrangements have already been made with the school and Laura is to begin her studies in February.

Since Laura will be past her eighteenth birthday by

the time she completes the course, this may pose a slight problem for us and I would explain how we are going to deal with it only I am afraid I am already late for prayers. I trust you had a restful summer.

Even before I finished reading that letter I knew that somehow Sister Margaret would talk the superintendent into letting us have all the money required for Laura out of "miscellaneous." As a matter of fact, I knew it the day we four talked in the cafeteria over an ash-bedecked and rather grimy table. Once more this extraordinary woman had come through for Laura and given her the break she needed.

The tables at last were turning, the strength of human kindness beginning to reshape the direction of an abused and forgotten life. Already Laura was looked at in a different way—no longer did she meet, as in those days when I had walked the streets of the neighborhood with her, those closed looks of distaste and fear, which are the lot of anyone ugly and misshapen, and which wound them so much. At last she was to have what she wanted—a chance to be useful in the best way she could express herself.

I walked down the steps of the Institution and out. There it stood, this massive gray gathering of stone and mortar surmounted by the protection of its wire and glass. How dreary it had looked the first day I had come here with Dorothy. That day seemed deeply distant. I seemed to have spent a whole lifetime within these walls, learning a great deal about humanity—and love. For whenever a child must suffer for something over which it has no control, all men end up suffering. To hurt a child is to hurt a man ten times over.

I went in and bought a paper from the old candy vendor of the past. He gave me a cheery "Good evening, Doc." A small child in a tartan skirt was carefully checking the phone coin return for a dime.

Outside the streets were brutal with sound. Either an eight-alarm fire squad or most of New York's Finest was due in this vicinity shortly. The sirens belled and yelled, red lights gyred wildly at an intersection ahead, and for a second they symbolized for me that moment long ago when Laura's charred body and soul had been plucked from confusion and terror and damnation and isolation, finally to be nurtured back to life and hope.

She needed all her strength to face this "jungle," as she had called it. I ducked my head into the wind as I passed the shops we had together gone by once, so slowly, with her arm through mine. METAL CEILINGS, and then the process server . . . DINETTE SETS . . . OPERARIAS . . . oh yes, SLIM'S PET SHOP, and, of course, COLD BEER.

Behind the confusion and the terror and the stone wall stood the defiance of human love. As I glanced back at the repellent edifice which housed such sheer dedication that it was almost an anachronism in our commercial, acquisitive society, it seemed to have over it another superscription than the "Abandon Hope" I had once imagined there: *"I am the door: by me if any man enter in, he shall be saved, and shall go in and out, and find pasture."*

It was a defiance of despair that had brought a disfigured girl out of helplessness and hopelessness. This small band of devoted women had formed a living phalanx of warriors between Laura and those forces in our world that, for some reason, always seem to push hardest against those who are weak, sick, poor, or in some way vulnerable. They were Sisters of Charity, indeed: "He who cares for the least of my brethren cares for me." And they had accomplished their task in the face of the necessarily burdensome aspects of institutional living, with all its protocol and procedures. Day after day they brought to children like Laura the care and love they needed, as if from some inexhaustible reservoir of emotional energy. Together with them, I had been privileged

Life

to conquer one silence at least. What inspired these contemporary heroines was another tale, no doubt buried deep in each individual life. There was now only one more page to turn in Laura's story before she left us.

29

It was nice to have good news to give Laura for once. She came into my office looking relaxed and well. Already the relief from pain in her legs was giving her a renewed confidence and delight in life.

Once more she started by talking about all the events of the summer that had so stirred her.

"All that time I felt so alive," she said. "The children got so tanned you don't know. And to think I'm soon going to graduate from high school. I can hardly believe it's really happening. You always told me never to look back, to look only to the future. And now I'm wondering what I'll do when I do graduate. I guess they'll find some sort of job for me, won't they? I know I have to leave here then."

"You're going to do a course in baby nursing," I said. "It's all been arranged for you, Laura."

She went quite pale. Her smile vanished and for a minute she was speechless as the full meaning of what I had said registered on her.

I had seen Laura react this way before. She, who had had so little in life, felt unworthy when confronted with compliments and presents, and once again this innate humility brought tears to her eyes, not of sadness, but of a gratitude so overwhelming that she couldn't cope with it properly. She looked definitely shocked, and then she rose to her feet, wiped her eyes, and said:

"I have to be dreaming. This can't be happening to me. You know, I'd given up all hope of ever becoming a nurse. I didn't want another disappointed dream, did I? Now you tell me that I'll have a chance to do the kind of work I want to, being with children. Is this real? Would you tell me again?"

I did so. Once more her feelings flooded her power to control them. In a dazed, bewildered way, as if out of nowhere, she asked, "Why are they so good to me here? It's important for me to know."

"They care for you, Laura. They want to give you the best they have."

"Do you mean they love me?" she persisted quietly, yet steadily. "Is that what love is?"

"I think it is."

"I've often wondered about love. The word is used so often, on TV, the movies, between boys and girls, but it seems to have so many different meanings. I guess it means to care for someone. My father married my mother. He must have loved her. They had me so they must have loved children. But that's a laugh, that's not true, is it? They hated me. Oh, why am I always so confused? I shouldn't think of anything but school. You ought to see the homework I have." She rolled her eyes expressively. "I'm going to work real hard, just you see."

She kept her promise and until January applied herself diligently to her schoolwork. She knew that in order to get into the nursing program she had to graduate from high school with good marks. She studied every single spare second she could find. Her efforts were not wasted, for she passed all her final examinations and was recommended for graduation.

Despite the pressure of study, Laura was full of happiness in those last months. She found time to help Sister Jean with another Christmas bonanza for the young ones, and then, when the time came, she was like any other girl about to graduate from high school—in a high state of excitement over her new dress and shoes. (The latter had her shopping every day for a week until she found just the pair she wanted.)

The day before graduation Laura came to see me and she was wearing her new clothes. In her white dress, high heels, and neatly combed fair hair she looked radiant, a clear-eyed young woman, vibrant with beauty, her skin softly glowing as if some flame were held behind her flesh. If the Institution had had a bell tower it would have been pealing in celebration.

Laura could scarcely contain herself, getting up, sitting down, insisting that I take a cigarette, and then insisting on lighting it for me, bubbling over with laughter one minute, crying the next.

"I still can't believe it's all really happening to me," she said. "But tomorrow at one-thirty I shall graduate. You're sure you like my shoes?" she asked suddenly, sticking them out with a critical frown.

"Very much," I said.

"Well, we're going to have a private ceremony in the principal's office. I was told I could bring three friends, people I cared about."

She paused a moment.

"Who did you choose, Laura?" I asked.

"I really wish they would let me bring everyone. It took me all last week to make up my mind, and yesterday I finally did."

"Yes?"

"I asked Sister Paulette," she said, ticking her off on the fingers of one hand.

"Of course."

"Then Mrs. Clancy, and I wasn't quite sure about the third person." Her eyes dropped. "I mean, I wanted to ask this person very much, but then I changed my mind and instead I invited my teacher. Would you sign my graduation album? Please do," she pressed impulsively. "I want you to write on the inside cover . . . that's a very special part of the book. I mean, it's the very first page and that's where I would like your name to be. I know you won't be in tomorrow, so that's why I brought the book down today."

"I'd be honored, Laura," I said, and while I got out my pen she rambled on, laughing.

"Mrs. Clancy and Sister Paulette are going to take me to lunch after graduation, and then in the evening the girls are all having a big party for me. Do you think I'll be able to eat anything after a late lunch?"

"I'm sure you will."

"I guess it's times like this when you really miss not being part of a family. Someday I want to have a family of my own and I'll make sure I go to my children's graduation. It means a lot to have your parents interested." Again her eyes strayed. "I miss them . . . wherever they are. Every once in a while I get sad like right now about that—not having a family, I mean—but I try always to remember what you told me, always to look forward, and that helps because, well, tomorrow is going to be just the very happiest day in my life. And I guess no one ever goes through life without some sort of sadness, do they? Oh, you always let me talk and talk and you never say very much. I used to think you did that on purpose so's I could hear myself."

The day we first heard your voice, Laura, I thought to myself, was another red-letter day within the Institution. It was I who had done the talking then. But she was off on another tack.

"Yes, I've learned a lot about me, but I don't understand others too well. With other people I feel like a stranger. When I think of leaving here, and being free, without any rules or anything, I get butterflies in my stomach. I really feel scared. How will I know what to do, whom to trust? Can you understand what I'm talking about?"

"Very well."

"I won't *feel* I'm alone, I'll *be* alone. It'll be for real; I'll be out there alone among all those thousands of people. That's more frightening than anything I know."

It was understandable enough. For Laura that moment was another severing. It was not only her childhood coming to an end, it was the separation from the only home she'd known.

Graduation day came and Laura rose to the occasion with everything she could muster. As might have been expected, both Mrs. Clancy and Sister Paulette cried as the principal awarded Laura her diploma. For this was more than an ordinary graduation for a high school girl; it was a personal accomplishment of high order, a victory over the forces of evil and the recovery of human waste.

After high school graduation she stayed on in the Institution, under Sister Margaret's celebrated "miscellaneous," attending the baby-nurse course. This took her to school for seven hours a day and the homework was heavy. I kept up my visits with her, though now these were mainly a matter of helping her understand the new studies that were being thrown at her from all sides. The physiology of birth, child-caring practices . . . Sister Philomene, her black bag bursting with little animals, pitched in with a special assist in biology, but some of the science work was pretty abstruse. A neighboring nurse was corralled to provide additional tutoring, and somehow, between us all, Laura survived the tough and intensive course of training.

By now she was no stranger to the challenges of competition, but by the end of the twelve-week course she was showing signs of strain. Would she pass the examinations?

"I feel so ignorant and stupid, as if my brain were dead," she said to me in a nadir of discouragement one day. "I know how to take care of babies and love them. But I'll never understand, not in a million years, why I have to know how the food in a child's stomach is broken down during digestion. Can you tell me what this has to do with feeding, bathing, and caring for the child? I really think I insulted the teacher today and I didn't want to do that. You see, she asked me why we burp infants. I told her it was to relieve the pressure of gas and make the child more comfortable. She wanted to know what was happening 'chemically' in the infant's stomach. I got mad and said what did it matter, chemically, so long as the infant burped! Oh well, I know I was wrong. I just can't seem to get the hang of all that technical stuff."

The day of the finals was a Friday. The results were due to be posted Monday at noon. I was to see her for the last time that afternoon, but I had decided to get there early and have a farewell lunch in the cafeteria with Sister Margaret and Mrs. Clancy. It was a windy day in late spring when I bought my paper from Abe, the newsstand vendor, and took the subway out. There was a headline about child abuse.

What with a couple of calls en route, I reached the Institution shortly after midday. I can only describe the atmosphere as like Sunday afternoon in the park when the home team wins the ball game and the only thing left to do is rip down the goal post. The excitement was vivid in the air, in the almost gay swirl of a nun's robe, and her quickly whispered "Have you heard . . . ?"

Laura had passed. Not only had she done so, but I learned at lunch that Sister Margaret had come through for her once again, managing to find a job for her in an institution that took care of little children. I was to see her at four o'clock.

But as I sat waiting at my desk I did not at first recognize the softly striding woman in white, wearing a nurse's cap and rubber-soled white shoes, at the far end of the hall. It was only when she was halfway down the passage that I saw that it was Laura and that she was smiling at me. She had come in the uniform she would wear for graduation in a few days' time. I suppose I saw for too long the shadow behind her, that of a small hunched child, scarred, ugly, and mute, clinging feebly to a nun for support.

"Hello, Laura," I said.

We sat and chatted about her plans, and the room she would occupy in a boarding house a short distance from her job, also procured by Sister Margaret. There were times when it was hard to believe that this glowing young person, with her sure smile and fulfilled flush of pleasure, was only eighteen. In those few years she had lived more lifetimes than is vouched to most human beings. The horror and the terror seemed already far in the past.

I imagine I must have stared at her just a little too long for she looked at me inquiringly. "Do you like my uniform?" she asked. "I put it on especially for you."

"Very much," I said. "You look fine, Laura."

Tears gathered in her eyes. (She had not lost that habit, at least!) She stood up abruptly.

"I guess you know I'm leaving next Monday, then. I'm so excited I hardly know how to think, but I'll be sorry to leave here, too. I don't really understand all that's happened to me, why I didn't speak, and all that . . . my illness. It seems too much. I don't know where to begin."

She looked about, as if avoiding my eyes or searching for words, or, perhaps, registering for the last time the features of this place where she had come to see me over so many years—I couldn't tell.

Then she said, "You have been the someone very special in my life. I'm not sure about it all, but every time I was desperate you comforted me. When I was confused you made things clear. When I needed someone to talk to, you were always there—even if you often said little. You're so many people wrapped into one. Oh, I don't know how to explain it. Somehow I know that whatever I have, well, you were responsible for my having it, but I can't tell how. I guess I can't put it into words. I don't know how I'm going to face life all alone."

"You'll do fine," I said.

She turned to me. "You know, I was asked to invite anyone I wanted to my graduation. Each time I thought about whom I'd ask, I kept thinking of you. I *almost* asked you when I graduated from high school," she said with a smile, "only each time I was about to, I got frightened.

250

Then I decided not to. Yes, it'd be better if I didn't give you a chance to answer. You see, I was so afraid you might refuse me and that would hurt me so much. I would much rather think that there was a chance you would have accepted than to know for sure my dream was hopeless." She hesitated, then said, "I wanted to remember you as someone who would never hurt me. . . . I do have one favor to ask before I leave. It may sound silly but it is important to me."

"Go ahead," I replied.

"May I hug you?"

"You may," I answered.

Laura put her arms around my neck and embraced me. Then she put me from her.

"You know," she said pensively, "I think you are going to miss me as much as I'm going to miss you."

She turned and with a firm stride left my office and my life, a diminishing white figure down the long familiar hallway until she vanished from my sight.

There were a few things for me to tidy up in this office I was now leaving for good, and I had some last farewells to pay. It was early evening by the time I left the Institution. Somehow I did not want to plunge into the bowels of the subway system at that moment and I found myself walking—walking and walking toward the great mass of building thrusting skyward, and already circled with winking lights.

This, then, is Laura's story. The coming of her voice, and the passing of it from my side, an absence that will somehow be there always.

But it is also the story of the fate that awaits each single child as a result of deprivation, poverty, and emotional illness. It is also the story of a group of mavericks who refused to give up. Forgotten, ignored, the nuns I had left toiled on. And as I walked ever more rapidly, their swirling robes were in my eyes, their voices whispering in my ears, "Doctor, there's Anne, and then there's Lorraine, too, if ever you thought you could . . ."

A chain-smoking, coffee-gorging social worker who refused to let a child deteriorate; no, I should not easily forget Mrs. Clancy. Nor Sister Paulette, who could cradle a child lost in the night to her bosom for hour after hour, and could weep true tears in imploring me to help her—her human voice would call me always.

And you, Sister Margaret, with your demure smile and inflexible will, which—I am perfectly sure—could move mountains at any required moment, I shall not forget you either. Whenever I hear the melodies of children at play, in their voices and vivid laughter I will hear your own, as you masterminded another hospital or city department. Heaven help the stock market if ever Sister Margaret moves into it!

I remembered that distant day when I had asked myself if nuns were people. I shook my head in memory. And as I walked toward the living city I sensed again that faint smell I had called "white" on my first visit to the Institution. I knew it now. It was milk. The milk of human kindness.